Greg Byrd, Lynn Byrd and Chris Pearce

Cambridge Checkpoint

Mathematics

Practice Book

8

CAMBRIDGE
UNIVERSITY PRESS

CAMBRIDGE
UNIVERSITY PRESS

University Printing House, Cambridge CB2 8BS, United Kingdom

One Liberty Plaza, 20th Floor, New York, NY 10006, USA

477 Williamstown Road, Port Melbourne, VIC 3207, Australia

4843/24, 2nd Floor, Ansari Road, Daryaganj, Delhi – 110002, India

79 Anson Road, #06–04/06, Singapore 079906

Cambridge University Press is part of the University of Cambridge.

It furthers the University's mission by disseminating knowledge in the pursuit of education, learning and research at the highest international levels of excellence.

www.cambridge.org
Information on this title: www.cambridge.org/9781107665996

© Cambridge University Press 2013

First published 2013

20 19 18 17 16 15 14

Printed in Great Britain by CPI Group (UK) Ltd, Croydon CR0 4YY

A catalogue record for this publication is available from the British Library

ISBN 978-1-107-66599-6 Paperback

Cover image © Cosmo Condina concepts / Alamy

Contents

Introduction

Welcome to Cambridge Checkpoint Mathematics Practice Book 8

The *Cambridge Checkpoint Mathematics* course covers the Cambridge Secondary 1 Mathematics framework.

The course is divided into three stages: 7, 8 and 9. This Practice Book can be used with Coursebook 8. It is intended to give you extra practice in all the topics covered in the Coursebook.

Like the Coursebook, the Practice Book is divided into 18 units. In each unit you will find an exercise for every topic. These exercises contain similar questions to the corresponding exercises in the Coursebook.

This Practice Book gives you a chance to try further questions on your own. This will improve your understanding of the subject. It will also help you to feel confident about working on your own when there is no teacher available to help you.

There are no explanations or worked examples in this book. If you are not sure what to do or need to remind yourself about something, look at the explanations and worked examples in the Coursebook.

1 Integers, powers and roots

◆ Exercise 1.1   Arithmetic with integers

1 Add these numbers.
   a $6 + -3$ **b** $-6 + -4$ **c** $-2 + -8$ **d** $-1 + 6$ **e** $-10 + 4$

2 Find the missing integer in each case.
   a $5 + \square = 2$ **b** $4 + \square = -6$ **c** $-3 + \square = 3$
   d $-12 + \square = -8$ **e** $7 + \square = -6$

3 Subtract.
   a $3 - 7$ **b** $-3 - 7$ **c** $-20 - 30$ **d** $5 - 15$ **e** $-9 - 4$

4 Subtract.
   a $4 - -6$ **b** $10 - -3$ **c** $-10 - -5$
   d $-6 - -12$ **e** $15 - -10$

> Add the inverse.

5 In each wall diagram, add the two numbers above to get the number below.
   For example, $3 + -5 = -2$. Find the bottom number in each diagram.

   a
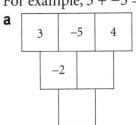

   b
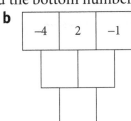

   c
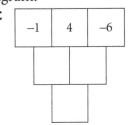

6 Copy this <u>multiplication</u> table.
   Fill in the missing numbers.

×	−3	−1	2	5
−3				
−1				
2				
5				25

7 Complete these divisions.
   a $20 \div -2$ **b** $-24 \div 3$ **c** $-44 \div -4$ **d** $28 \div -4$ **e** $-12 \div -6$

8 Look at the multiplication in the box.
   Use the same integers to write down two divisions.

   $-5 \times 6 = -30$

9 Xavier has made a mistake.
   Correct it.

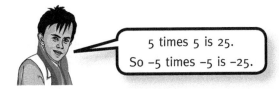

> 5 times 5 is 25.
> So −5 times −5 is −25.

10 The product of two different integers is -16. What could they be?

11 Find the missing numbers.
   a $-2 \times \square = 20$ **b** $4 \times \square = -12$ **c** $\square \times 9 = -45$ **d** $\square \times -5 = -35$

1 Find the first three multiples of each number.
   a 12   **b** 15   **c** 32   **d** 50

2 From the numbers in the box, find:
   a a multiple of 10   **b** two factors of 24
   c a common factor of 27 and 36   **d** a prime number.

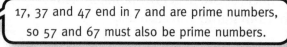

| 8 | 9 | 12 | 23 | 32 | 40 |

3 List all the prime numbers between 40 and 50.

4 Which of the numbers in the box is:
   a a multiple of 2
   b a multiple of 5
   c a common multiple of 2 and 5
   d a factor of 500
   e a prime number
   f a common multiple of 2 and 3?

| 95 | 96 | 97 | 98 | 99 | 100 |

You may use some numbers more than once.

5 Is Mia correct?

17, 37 and 47 end in 7 and are prime numbers, so 57 and 67 must also be prime numbers.

6 Write true (T) or false (F) for each statement.
   a 7 is a factor of 84.
   b 80 is a multiple of 15.
   c There is only one prime number between 90 and 100.
   d 36 is the lowest common multiple (LCM) of 6 and 9.
   e 5 is the highest common factor (HCF) of 25 and 50.

7 Find the LCM of each pair of numbers.
   a 4 and 6   **b** 15 and 20   **c** 20 and 50   **d** 6 and 7

8 Find the factors of each number.
   a 27   **b** 28   **c** 72   **d** 82   **e** 31

9 Find the <u>prime</u> factors of each number.
   a 32   **b** 18   **c** 70   **d** 99   **e** 19

10 Find the HCF of each pair.
   a 12 and 15   **b** 12 and 18   **c** 12 and 24   **d** 12 and 25

11 The HCF of 221 and 391 is 17.
   Explain why 221 and 391 cannot be prime numbers.

12 Find two numbers that are <u>not</u> prime and have a HCF of 1.

1 Copy and complete these factor trees.

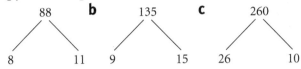

  a 88
  8   11

  b 135
  9   15

  c 260
  26   10

2 **a** Draw two different factor trees for 80.
  b Write 80 as a product of primes.

3 Write down each number.
  a $2 \times 3^2 \times 5^2$ **b** $2^4 \times 3^3$ **c** $2^2 \times 11^2$

4 $84 = 2^2 \times 3 \times 7$ and $90 = 2 \times 3^2 \times 5$
  a Write the HCF of 84 and 90 as a product of primes.
  b Write the LCM of 84 and 90 as a product of primes.

5 **a** Write each number as a product of primes.
     i 120   **ii** 160
  b Find the LCM of 120 and 160.
  c Find the HCF of 120 and 160.

 6 **a** Find the HCF of 84 and 96.
  b Find the LCM of 84 and 96.

 7 **a** Find the HCF of 104 and 156.
  b Find the LCM of 104 and 156.

 8 $10 = 2 \times 5$ $100 = 2^2 \times 5^2$ $1000 = 2^3 \times 5^3$
  Write 10 000 as a product of primes.

 9

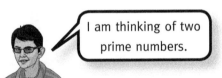

I am thinking of two prime numbers.

I can tell you their HCF.

I can tell you how to find their LCM.

  a How can Sasha do that?
  b What will Razi tell Jake?

10 **a** Write 81 as a product of primes.
   b Write 154 as a product of primes.
   c Explain why the HCF of 81 and 154 must be 1.

◆ Exercise 1.4 Powers and roots

1 Find the value of each of these.

  a 2^3 **b** 3^3 **c** 4^3 **d** 5^3 **e** 10^3

2 Find the value of each of these.

  a 2^4 **b** 3^4 **c** 4^4 **d** 10^4

3 a 4^4 is equal to 2^N. What number is N?

  b 9^3 is equal to 3^M. What number is M?

4 The number 100 has two square roots.

  a What is their sum?   **b** What is their product?

5 Find the square roots of each number.

  a 1   **b** 36   **c** 169   **d** 256   **e** 361

 6 a Show that $\dfrac{3^3-1}{2} = 3^2 + 3 + 1$.

  b Show that $\dfrac{4^3-1}{3} = 4^2 + 4 + 1$.

  c Write a similar expression involving 5^3.

 7 The numbers in the box are all identical in value.
Use this fact to write down:

  a $\sqrt{4096}$ **b** $\sqrt[3]{4096}$.

| 2^{12} | 4^6 | 16^3 | 64^2 | 4096 |

8 Find the value of:

  a $\sqrt{121}$ **b** $\sqrt{289}$ **c** $\sqrt{400}$ **d** $\sqrt{1}$.

9 Find the value of:

  a $\sqrt[3]{8}$ **b** $\sqrt[3]{125}$ **c** $\sqrt[3]{27}$ **d** $\sqrt[3]{1000}$

10 $11^3 = 1331$. Use this fact to work out:

  a 11^4 **b** $\sqrt[3]{1331}$.

11 Explain why Alicia is correct.

A square root of 25 could be less than a square root of 16.

2 Sequences, expressions and formulae

◆ Exercise 2.1 Generating sequences

1 Write down the first three terms of each sequence.
   a first term: 3   term-to-term rule: 'add 2'
   b first term: 2   term-to-term rule: 'subtract 2'
   c first term: 3   term-to-term rule: 'add 5'
   d first term: -1 term-to-term rule: 'subtract 5'
   e first term: -10 term-to-term rule: 'add 20'
   f first term: -100 term-to-term rule: 'subtract 20'

2 The first term of a sequence is 10. The term-to-term rule is 'add 5'.
   What is the sixth term of the sequence? Explain how you worked out your answer.

3 The first term of a sequence is 5. The term-to-term rule is 'add 10'.
   What is the 20th term of the sequence? Explain how you worked out your answer.

4 The fifth term of a sequence is 23. The term-to-term rule is 'add 4'.
   Work out the first term of the sequence. Explain how you solved the problem.

5 The 10th term of a sequence is 35. The term-to-term rule is 'add 3'.
   Work out the fifth term of the sequence. Explain how you solved the problem.

6 The 10th term of a sequence is 20. The term-to-term rule is 'subtract 4'.
   Work out the fifth term of the sequence. Explain how you solved the problem.

7 The eighth term of a sequence is 19; the seventh term of the sequence is 16.
   Work out the fifth term of the sequence. Explain how you solved the problem.

8 The table shows two of the terms in a sequence.

Position number	1	2	4	8	50
Term		1			49

   Position-to-term rule: term = position number $- 1$
   Use the position-to-term rule to work out the missing numbers from the sequence.
   Copy and complete the table.

9 Use the position-to-term rule to work out the first four terms of each sequence.
   a term = $2 \times$ position number   **b** term = position number $+ 10$
   c term = $2 \times$ position number $+ 3$ **d** term = $3 \times$ position number $- 2$

10 Use the position-to-term rules to work out: **i** the 10th term   **ii** the 20th term of each sequence.
   a term = position number $+ 100$ **b** term = $10 \times$ position number
   c term = $5 \times$ position number $+ 10$ **d** term = $5 \times$ position number $- 10$

11 The third term of a sequence is 13. The eighth term of the sequence is 38.
   Which of these position-to-term rules is the correct one for the sequence?
   Show how you worked out your answer.

A term = position number $+ 10$	**B** term = $4 \times$ position number $+ 1$
C term = $5 \times$ position number $- 2$	**D** term = $6 \times$ position number $- 5$

1 For each sequence of numbers:
  i write down the term-to-term rule
  ii write the sequence of numbers in a table
  iii work out the position-to-term rule
  iv check your rule works for the first three terms.
  a 3, 6, 9, 12, …, …   **b** 3, 5, 7, 9, …, …   **c** 3, 9, 15, 21, …, …

2 Work out the position-to-term rule for each sequence of numbers.
  a 6, 12, 18, 24, …, …   **b** 7, 10, 13, 16, …, …   **c** 8, 18, 28, 38, …, …

3 For each sequence of numbers:
  i write down the term-to-term rule
  ii write the sequence of numbers in a table
  iii work out the position-to-term rule
  iv check your rule works for the first three terms.
  a 2, 3, 4, 5, …, …   **b** 12, 13, 14, 15, …, …   **c** 22, 23, 24, 25, …, …

4 Work out the position-to-term rule for each sequence of numbers.
  a 5, 6, 7, 8, …, …   **b** 25, 26, 27, 28, …, …   **c** 125, 126, 127, 128, …, …

5 This pattern is made from grey squares.

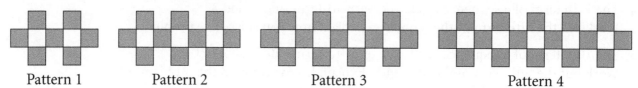

Pattern 1   Pattern 2   Pattern 3   Pattern 4

  a Write down the sequence of the numbers of grey squares.
  b Write down the term-to-term rule.
  c Explain how the sequence is formed.
  d Work out the position-to-term rule.

6 This sequence of shapes is made from squares.

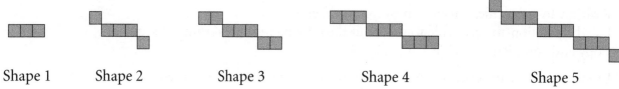

Shape 1   Shape 2   Shape 3   Shape 4   Shape 5

  a Draw shape 6.
  b Work out the position-to-term rule.

◆ Exercise 2.3 Using the *n*th term

1 Work out the first three terms and the 10th term of the sequences with the *n*th term given to you below.

   a $n + 4$ **b** $2n$ **c** $2n + 4$
   d $n - 2$ **e** $3n$ **f** $3n - 2$

2 This pattern is made from circles.

  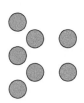 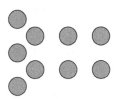

Pattern 1   Pattern 2   Pattern 3   Pattern 4

   a Write down the sequence of the numbers of circles.
   b Write down the term-to-term rule.
   c Explain how the sequence is formed.
   d Work out the position-to-term rule.
   e Copy and complete the workings to check that the *n*th term, $2n + 1$, works for the first four terms.

      1st term = $2 \times 1 + 1 = 3$ 2nd term = $2 \times \square + 1 = \square$
      3rd term = $2 \times \square + 1 = \square$ 4th term = $2 \times \square + 1 = \square$

3 This pattern is made from squares.

   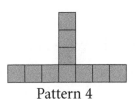

Pattern 1   Pattern 2   Pattern 3   Pattern 4

   a Explain how the sequence is formed.
   b Work out the position-to-term rule.

 4 This sequence is made from squares.

 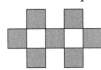 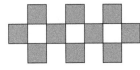 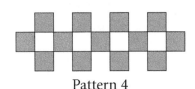

Pattern 1   Pattern 2   Pattern 3   Pattern 4

Anders thinks that the *n*th term for the sequence of numbers of squares is $n + 3$.
Anders is wrong.

   a What errors has Anders made?
   b What is the correct *n*th term? Explain how you worked out your answer.

1 a Copy and complete the table of values for each function machine.

i

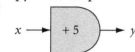

x	1	2	3	4
y				

ii

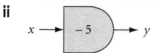

x	5	6	7	8
y				

b Draw mapping diagrams for each of the functions in part **a**.

c Write each of the functions in part **a** as an equation.

2 a Copy and complete the table of values for each function machine.

> When you are given a *y*-value and need to work out the *x*-value, work backwards through the function machine.

i

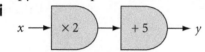

x	1	2	3	4
y				

ii

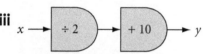

x	2	5		20
y			17	

iii

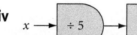

x	2		10	
y		13		25

iv

x	5		40	
y		−1		7

b Write each of the functions in part **a** as an equation.

3 a Work out the rule for each function machine.

i

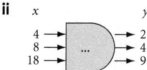

x   y

5 → 0
10 → ... → 5
15 → 10

ii

x   y

4 → 2
8 → ... → 4
18 → 9

b Write each of the functions in part **a** as an equation.

4 Work out the equation of this function machine.

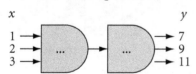

x   y

1 → 7
2 → ... → ... → 9
3 → 11

Explain how you worked out your answer.

5 Hassan and Maha look at this function machine.

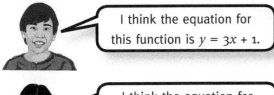

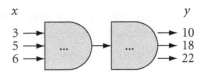

Which of them is correct? Explain your answer.

 6 Work out the equation of this function machine.

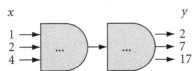

Explain how you worked out your answer.

Exercise 2.5 Constructing linear expressions

1 Zalika has a box that contains c one-dollar coins.
Write an expression for the total number of one-dollar coins she has in the box when:
  a she takes 2 out
  b she puts in 10 more
  c she takes out half of the coins
  d she takes out a quarter of the coins
  e she doubles the number of coins in the box and adds an extra 5.

> If she takes out a quarter, what fraction does she have left?

2 Shen thinks of a number, n.
Write an expression for the number Shen gets when he:
  a multiplies the number by 2 then adds 7
  b divides the number by 3 then adds 6.

3 The price of one bag of flour is $\$f$.
The price of one bag of sugar is $\$s$.
The price of one bag of raisins is $\$r$.
Write an expression for the total cost of:
  a four bags of flour and one bag of raisins
  b 12 bags of flour, three bags of sugar and two bags of raisins.

 4 Ahmad thinks of a number, n. He adds 4 then multiplies the result by 3.
Which of these expressions is the correct expression for Ahmad's number? Explain your answer.

  A $n + 12$ **B** $n + 4 \times 3$ **C** $4 + n \times 3$ **D** $3(n + 4)$ **E** $n(4 \times 3)$

5 Tanesha thinks of a number, n. Write down an expression for the number Tanesha gets when she subtracts 5 from the number, then multiplies the result by 2.

1 Work out the value of the expression:

a $a + 3$ when $a = 7$

b $b + 6$ when $b = -4$

c $3c$ when $c = -3$

d $\frac{d}{5}$ when $d = -35$

e $a + b$ when $a = 3$ and $b = -5$

f $c - d$ when $c = 14$ and $d = 7$

g $5e + 2f$ when $e = 3$ and $f = 5$

h $2g + h$ when $g = 9$ and $h = -20$

i $3x - 7$ when $x = -5$

j $10 - 2x$ when $x = 6$

k $\frac{x}{4} - 10$ when $x = 20$

l $\frac{x}{2} + \frac{y}{10}$ when $x = 30$ and $y = -30$.

2 Work out the value of the expression:

a $a^2 - 6$ when $a = 4$

b $30 - b^2$ when $b = 6$

c $a^2 + b^2$ when $a = 3$ and $b = 4$

d $c^2 - d^2$ when $c = 5$ and $d = 6$

e $3p^2$ when $p = 4$

f $5q^2 + 1$ when $q = 10$

g t^3 when $t = 2$

h $10v^3$ when $v = 4$

i $z^3 - 2$ when $z = 2$

j $100 - w^3$ when $w = 5$

k $\frac{r^2}{2}$ when $r = 8$

l $\frac{s^3}{10}$ when $s = 10$

m $m^2 + 3$ when $m = -4$

n $5n^3$ when $n = -2$.

> Remember that t^3 means $t \times t \times t$.

3 a Write a formula for the number of seconds in any number of minutes, using:

i words **ii** letters.

b Use your formula from part **a** to work out the number of seconds in 30 minutes.

4 Use the formula $d = 16t^2$ to work out d when $t = 2$.

5 Use the formula $V = \frac{Ah}{3}$ to work out V when $A = 6$ and $h = 4$.

> Remember that Ah means $A \times h$.

6 Use the formula $A = \frac{(a+b)}{2} \times h$ to work out A when $a = 5$, $b = 7$ and $h = 4$.

7 Harsha uses this formula to work out the volume of a triangular-based pyramid:

$V = \frac{blh}{6}$, where V is the volume, b is the base width, l is the base length and h is the height.

> Remember that blh means $b \times l \times h$.

Harsha compares two pyramids.
Pyramid A has a base width of 4 cm, base length of 3 cm and height of 16 cm.
Pyramid B has a base width of 6 cm, base length of 4 cm and height of 8 cm.
Which pyramid has the larger volume? Show your working.

8 Chaan knows that his company uses this formula to work out how much to pay its employees:
$P = rh + b$, where P is the pay (\$), r = rate of pay per hour, h = hours worked and b = bonus.
Chaan's boss paid him \$12.55 per hour. Last week he earned a bonus of \$45 and his pay was \$547.
His working to find out how many hours he has been paid for is shown below.
Chaan now has to solve this equation:
$547 = 12.55h + 45$
Work out the equation that Chaan needs to solve when his pay is \$477.25 for the week, including a \$38 bonus.

P = rh + b

Substitute P = \$547, r = \$12.55, b = \$45.

\$547 = \$12.55 × h + \$45

Simplify: 547 = 12.55h + 45

3 Place value, ordering and rounding

◆ Exercise 3.1   Multiplying and dividing by 0.1 and 0.01

1 Write each number in: **i** figures   **ii** words.
   a 10^2 **b** 10^4 **c** 10^8 **d** 10^9

2 Write each number as a power of 10.
   a 10   **b** 1 000 000   **c** 1000   **d** 10 000 000

3 Work these out.
   a 33×0.1 **b** 999×0.1 **c** 30×0.1 **d** 8.7×0.1
   e 77×0.01 **f** 70×0.01 **g** 700×0.01 **h** 7×0.01

4 Work these out.
   a $5 \div 0.1$ **b** $5.6 \div 0.1$ **c** $55.6 \div 0.1$ **d** $0.55 \div 0.1$
   e $5 \div 0.01$ **f** $5.6 \div 0.01$ **g** $55.6 \div 0.01$ **h** $0.55 \div 0.01$

5 Work out the answers to these questions.
   Use inverse operations to check your answers.
   a 27×0.1 **b** 27.9×0.01 **c** $0.2 \div 0.1$ **d** $2.7 \div 0.01$

6 Which symbol, $\times$ or $\div$, goes in each box?
   a $55 \boxed{} 0.1 = 550$ **b** $46 \boxed{} 0.01 = 0.46$ **c** $3.7 \boxed{} 0.1 = 37$
   d $208 \boxed{} 0.01 = 2.08$ **e** $0.19 \boxed{} 0.1 = 1.9$ **f** $505 \boxed{} 0.01 = 5.05$

7 What goes in the box, 0.1 or 0.01?
   a $44 \times \boxed{} = 4.4$ **b** $4.4 \div \boxed{} = 44$ **c** $0.40 \times \boxed{} = 0.004$
   d $4 \div \boxed{} = 40$ **e** $44.4 \times \boxed{} = 0.444$ **f** $44 \div \boxed{} = 4400$

8 One of these calculations, **A**, **B**, **C** or **D**, gives a different answer to the other three. Which one?
   Show your working.

   A $0.096 \div 0.1$ **B** 96×0.01 **C** 9.6×0.1 **D** $96 \div 0.01$

9 Alicia thinks of a number. She divides her number by 0.01, and then multiplies the answer by 0.1.
   She then divides this answer by 0.01 and gets a final answer of 2340.
   What number does Alicia think of first?

10 This is part of Ceri's homework.

> _Question_ 'When you multiply a number with one decimal place by 0.01
>   you will always get an answer that is smaller than zero.'
>   Write down one example to show that this statement is not true.
> _Answer_ $345.8 \times 0.01 = 3.458$ and 3.458 is not smaller than zero so the
>   statement is not true.

For each of these statements, write down one example to show that it is not true.
   a When you divide a number with one decimal place by 0.1 you will always get an answer that is
   bigger than 1.
   b When you multiply a number with two decimal places by 0.01 you will always get an answer that
   is greater than 0.01.

1 Write the decimal numbers in each set in order of size, starting with the smallest.

    a 7.36, 3.76, 6.07, 7.63   **b** 8.03, 3.08, 8.11, 5.99

    c 23.4, 19.44, 23.05, 19.42   **d** 1.08, 2.11, 1.3, 1.18

    e 45.454, 45.545, 45.399, 45.933   **f** 5.183, 5.077, 50.44, 5.009

    g 31.425, 31.148, 31.41, 31.14   **h** 7.502, 7.052, 7.02, 7.2

2 Write the measurements in each set in order of size, starting with the smallest.

    a 4.3 cm, 27 mm, 0.2 cm, 7 mm   **b** 34.5 cm, 500 mm, 29 cm, 19.5 mm

    c 2000 g, 75.75 kg, 5550 g, 3 kg   **d** 1.75 kg, 1975 g, 0.9 kg, 1800 g

    e 0.125 l, 100 ml, 0.2 l, 150 ml   **f** 25 km, 2750 m, 0.05 km, 999 m

    g 50 000 g, 0.75 t, 850 kg, 359 999 g, 57.725 kg, 1.001 t, 500 kg, 200 g

3 Write the correct sign, < or >, between each pair of numbers.

    a 7.28 ☐ 7.34   **b** 9.1 ☐ 9.03   **c** 0.33 ☐ 0.04

    d 56.4 ☐ 56.35   **e** 0.66 ☐ 0.606   **f** 3.505 ☐ 3.7

    g 0.77 t ☐ 806 kg   **h** 7800 m ☐ 0.8 km   **i** 3.5 kg ☐ 375 g

    j 0.125 m ☐ 15 cm   **k** 156.3 cm ☐ 1234 mm   **l** 0.5 l ☐ 700 ml

4 Write the correct sign, = or ≠, between each pair of measurements.

    a 205.5 cm ☐ 255 mm   **b** 0.125 l ☐ 125 ml   **c** 500 g ☐ 0.05 kg

    d 2.7 l ☐ 27 ml   **e** 0.05 m ☐ 50 mm   **f** 10.5 t ☐ 1050 kg

    g 0.22 kg ☐ 220 g   **h** 1.75 km ☐ 175 m   **i** 0.125 m ☐ 125 cm

5 Frank and Sarina run around a park every day. They keep a record of the distances they run each day for 10 days.
These are the distances that Frank runs each day.

    400 m, 2.4 km, 0.8 km, 3200 m, 32 km, 1.2 km, 1.6 m, 2000 m, 3.6 km, 1.5 km

  a Which distances do you think Frank has written down incorrectly? Explain your answers.

These are the distances that Sarina jogs each day.

    2 km, 4000 m, 0.75 km, 3.5 km, 1000 m, 3000 m, 1.25 km, 0.5 km, 3250 m, 1.75 km

  b Sarina says that the longest distance she ran is almost ten times the shortest distance she ran. Is Sarina correct? Explain your answer.

Frank and Sarina run in different parks.
The distance round one of the parks is 250 m. The distance round the other park is 400 m.
Frank and Sarina always run a whole number of times around their park.

  c Who do you think runs in the 250 m park? Explain how you made your decision.

6 Rearrange the digits on the four cards to make as many decimal numbers as possible.

    ☐ 1 ☐ ☐ 2 ☐ ☐ 3 ☐ ☐ . ☐

> There are more than ten numbers to find.

Put all your numbers in order, starting with the smallest.

◆ Exercise 3.3 Rounding

1 Round each number to the given degree of accuracy.
   a 13 (nearest 10)
   b 428 (nearest 10)
   c 505 (nearest 100)
   d 261 (nearest 100)
   e 7531 (nearest 1000)
   f 35 432 (nearest 1000)
   g 71 177 (nearest 10 000)
   h 345 432 (nearest 10 000)
   i 750 000 (nearest 100 000)
   j 37 489 504 (nearest 100 000)
   k 37 489 504 (nearest 1 000 000)
   l 89 499 555 (nearest million)

2 Round each number to the given degree of accuracy.
   a 83.4 (nearest whole number)
   b 59.501 (nearest whole number)
   c 0.377 (nearest whole number)
   d 523.815 (one decimal place)
   e 37.275 (one decimal place)
   f 0.983 (one decimal place)
   g 0.0543 (two decimal places)
   h 2.725 (two decimal places)
   i 59.995 (two decimal places)

3 For each part, write whether **A**, **B** or **C** is the correct answer.
   a 5299 rounded to the nearest 10
      A 5290   **B** 5300   **C** 5310
   b 72 220 rounded to the nearest 100
      A 72 000   **B** 80 000   **C** 72 200
   c 549 750 rounded to the nearest 10 000
      A 550 000   **B** 500 000   **C** 600 000
   d 7.97 rounded to one decimal place
      A 8   **B** 8.0   **C** 7.10
   e 48.595 rounded to two decimal places
      A 48.6   **B** 48.60   **C** 48.59
   f 10.999 rounded to two decimal places
      A 11   **B** 11.0   **C** 11.00

4 For each answer, write down whether it is correct or not.
   If it is incorrect, write down what mistake has been made and give the correct
   answer to the question.
   a 17.05 rounded to the nearest whole number is 17.0
   b 12 399 rounded to the nearest 10 is 12 400
   c 37 548 rounded to the nearest 1000 is 38 000
   d 45.996 rounded to two decimal places is 45.00
   e 39.9501 rounded to one decimal place is 39.9

◆ Exercise 3.4 Adding and subtracting decimals

1 Work these out.
- **a** 7.36 + 7.36
- **b** 38.38 + 27.27
- **c** 4.78 + 8.74
- **d** 18.96 + 2.14
- **e** 0.77 + 5.38
- **f** 76.767 + 9.5
- **g** 32.22 + 0.977
- **h** 13.809 + 8.37

2 Work these out.
- **a** 7.45 − 4.33
- **b** 27.58 − 8.36
- **c** 44.73 − 3.55
- **d** 21.66 − 6.67
- **e** 8.75 − 2.85
- **f** 45.6 − 5.49
- **g** 57.37 − 45.6
- **h** 12.42 − 8.765

3 Work these out.
- **a** 36 − 4.3
- **b** 43 − 8.3
- **c** 58 − 9.55
- **d** 106 − 68.22

4 The Statue of Liberty was a gift from France to America.
It was completed in 1886.
The monument consists of a foundation, a pedestal and
a statue on the top.
The height of the foundation is 19.81 m.
The height of the pedestal is 27.13 m.
The height of the statue is 46.3 m.
What is the total height of the Statue of Liberty?

5 The table shows the progression of the women's high
jump world records.
Is the difference in the world record height jumped
between 1930 and 1960 larger than the difference in
the world record height jumped between 1960 and 1990?
Show how you worked out your answer.

Year	Height (m)
1930	1.605
1960	1.86
1990	2.09

◆ Exercise 3.5 Dividing decimals

1 Work out these divisions.
Give your answers correct to one decimal place.

   a $33 \div 2$ **b** $44 \div 3$ **c** $55 \div 4$

   d $66 \div 9$ **e** $911 \div 6$ **f** $911 \div 7$

   g $911 \div 8$ **h** $911 \div 9$ **i** $119 \div 9$

2 Work out these divisions.
Give your answers correct to two decimal places.

   a $10.98 \div 10$ **b** $98.7 \div 9$ **c** $8.76 \div 8$

   d $76.5 \div 7$ **e** $0.654 \div 6$ **f** $5.43 \div 5$

   g $4.32 \div 4$ **h** $0.321 \div 3$ **i** $2.19 \div 2$

3 A machine cuts a 15.6 m length of plastic into eight equal pieces.
How long is each piece?

4 A machine shares 2.6 kg of metal balls equally into six containers.
What weight of metal balls is in each container?
Give your answer correct to two decimal places.

5 A piece of A4 paper is 29.7 cm long.
It is folded in half across its length. Then it is folded in half again, in the same direction.
What is the length of each quarter of the piece of A4 paper?
Give your answer correct to two decimal places.

6 A piece of A5 paper is 14.8 cm wide.
It is folded to give seven equally wide pieces.
How wide is each piece?
Give your answer correct to one decimal place.

7 Four friends go food shopping for a barbeque.
They visit three shops.
They spend $12.25 in one, $2.49 in the second and $18.18 in the last.
They share the total cost of the shopping equally among them.
How much do they each pay?

8 A machine mixes four different chemicals to make large plastic containers.
It uses 7.2 kg of chemical A, 5.3 kg of chemical B, 1.25 kg of chemical C and 0.275 kg of chemical D.
The machine produces six identical containers from the chemicals.
How much does each large plastic container weigh?
Give your answer correct to two decimal places.

◆ Exercise 3.6　Multiplying by decimals

1 This is part of Ahmad's homework.

> *Question* *Use an equivalent calculation to work out 4.29 × 0.3*
> *Answer* *As 0.3 = 3 ÷ 10*
> *I can work out 4.29 × 3 × 10 instead*
>
>   4.²2 9
>   × 3
>   ─────
>   1 2. 6 7
>
> *12.67 × 10 = <u>126.7</u>*

a Ahmad has made several mistakes. What are they?
b Use an equivalent calculation to work out the correct answer to 4.29 × 0.3.

2 This is part of Harsha's homework.

> *Question* *Use an equivalent calculation to work out 31 × 0.08*
> *Answer* *As 0.08 = 80 ÷ 100*
> *I can work out 31 × 80 ÷ 100 instead*
>
>   31
>   × 80
>   ─────
>   2480
>
> *2480 ÷ 100 = <u>24.80</u>*

a Harsha has made several mistakes. What are they?
b Use an equivalent calculation to work out the correct answer to 31 × 0.08.

3 Use an equivalent calculation to work out each part.
　a 2.3×0.2　**b** 2.73×0.3　**c** 6.06×0.4
　d 4.85×0.5　**e** 4.85×0.05　**f** 6.24×0.06
　g 3.6×0.07　**h** 7.3×0.08　**i** 62.4×0.09

4 Use equivalent calculations to work these out.
　a 12×0.9　**b** 24×0.8　**c** 36×0.7
　d 408×0.6　**e** 50×0.05　**f** 13×0.02
　g 24×0.03　**h** 35×0.04　**i** 406×0.05

5 Use the written method you prefer to work these out.
　a 24.6×0.3　**b** 25.9×0.04　**c** 1.88×0.7　**d** 0.92×0.05

6 Which is larger: 0.2×43.6 or 96.8×0.09?
　Show your working.

7 Show that 0.4×8491.3 metres is approximately equal to 3.4 kilometres.

◆ Exercise 3.7   Dividing by decimals

1 This is part of Jake's homework.

> _Question_ _Use an equivalent calculation to work out 24 ÷ 0.4_
> _Answer_   _As 0.4 = 4 ÷ 10_
>   _I can work out (24 × 4) ÷ 10 instead_
>   ³28
>   × 4
>   ───
>   112
>   112 ÷ 10 = 11.2

a Jake has made a mistake. What is it?
b Use an equivalent calculation to work out the correct answer to 24 ÷ 0.4

2 This is part of Maha's homework.

> _Question_ _Use an equivalent calculation to work out 35.4 ÷ 0.06_
> _Answer_   _As 0.06 = 0.6 ÷ 100_
>   _I can work out (35.4 × 100) ÷ 0.6 instead_
>   _As 35.4 × 100 = 3540_
>   _3540 ÷ 0.6 = (3540 × 10) ÷ 6_
>   _As 3540 × 10 = 35400_
>   5900
>   6 ⟌ 35400
>   _So 35.4 ÷ 0.06 = 5900_

a Maha has made several mistakes. What are they?
b Use an equivalent calculation to work out the correct answer to 35.4 ÷ 0.06

3 Use an equivalent calculation to work out each part.
   a $12 \div 0.2$ **b** $21 \div 0.3$ **c** $24 \div 0.4$
   d $30 \div 0.5$ **e** $3.6 \div 0.6$ **f** $48.6 \div 0.9$
   g $31.2 \div 0.8$ **h** $4.2 \div 0.7$ **i** $459 \div 0.6$

4 Use equivalent calculations to work these out.
   a $22 \div 0.02$ **b** $36 \div 0.04$ **c** $42 \div 0.06$
   d $24 \div 0.08$ **e** $1.6 \div 0.08$ **f** $5.4 \div 0.09$
   g $497 \div 0.07$ **h** $5.3 \div 0.05$ **i** $113.4 \div 0.03$

5 Use the written method you prefer to work these out.
   a $23.5 \div 0.4$ correct to one decimal place   **b** $19.1 \div 0.6$ correct to one decimal place
   c $23.5 \div 0.8$ correct to two decimal places   **d** $613 \div 0.03$ correct to two decimal places

6 Work out $(18.6 - 9.88) \div (0.35 \times 2)$. Give your answer correct to two decimal places.

◆ Exercise 3.8 Estimating and approximating

1 Work out an estimate for each of these.

  a $72 + 29$ **b** $623 - 493$ **c** $82 \div 22$ **d** 477×31

2 Zalika has completed her homework.

  a $589 + 424 = 1013$
  b $74 - 46 = 28$
  c $928 \div 32 \approx 29$
  d $47 \times 24 = 1128$

For each part of her homework:
  i use estimates to check the answers
  ii use inverse operations to check the answers.

In questions 3 to 6:
  i work out the answer to the problem
  ii show all your working and at each step explain what it is that you have worked out
  iii make sure your working is clearly and neatly presented
  iv check your answer using estimation or inverse operations.

3 Jimmi works for a local supermarket.
He collects the shopping trolleys every evening.
He earns 20 cents for each trolley he returns to
the supermarket.
In one week he collects the number of trolleys shown.
How much money will Jimmi be paid this week?
Give your answer to the nearest dollar.

Trolleys collected:
Monday 63   Tuesday 47
Wednesday 23   Thursday 67
Friday 79   Saturday 122

4 Max is an electrician. For each job he does he charges $28 an hour <u>plus</u> a fee of $30.
  a Max does a job for Mr Field. It takes him $3\frac{1}{2}$ hours.
     How much does he charge Mr Field?
  b Max charges Mrs Li a total of $65.
     How long did the job for Mrs Li take?
     Give your answer in hours and minutes.

5 Belinda is going to buy a car.
She sees the car she wants in a show room. It costs $17 995.
Belinda can use either cash or a payment plan to buy the car.
The payment plan requires a first payment of $4995 followed by 36 monthly payments of $420.
How much more will it cost Belinda if she buys the car using the payment plan rather than cash?

6 Dylan sells luxury muffins to a local shop.
He bakes 70 luxury muffins a day, five days a week.
He does this for 46 weeks a year.
The shop owner pays Dylan $4.75 for four luxury muffins.
How much money should Dylan make from selling his luxury muffins in one year?

4 Length, mass and capacity

Exercise 4.1 Choosing suitable units

1 Which metric unit would you use to measure each of these?
  a the height of a mountain
  b the width of a book
  c the mass of a ship
  d the mass of a mobile phone
  e the capacity of a mug
  f the capacity of a paddling pool

2 Which metric unit would you use to measure each of these?
  a the area of a country
  b the area of a computer screen
  c the volume of a room
  d the volume of a pencil case

3 Write down whether you think each of these measurements is true (**T**) or false (**F**).
  a The volume of a swimming pool is 100 m³.
  b The length of desk is 120 mm.
  c The mass of an elephant is 1 tonne.
  d The capacity of a large spoon is 2 litres.
  e The area of a football field is 150 m².
  f The height of a house is 3 m.

4 Adrian estimates that the height of his car is 2.5 m.
Is this a reasonable estimate?
Give a reason for your answer.

5 Sasha estimates that the mass of one of her friends is 65 kg.
Is this a reasonable estimate?
Give a reason for your answer.

6 Humi's car breaks down and it takes him 3 hours to walk back to his house.
He estimates that the distance he walked was 30 km.
Is this a reasonable estimate?
Give a reason for your answer.

7 Maha has two brothers, Alan and Zac.
Maha knows that Alan has a mass of 22.5 kg.
She estimates that Zac's mass is three times Alan's mass.
Work out an estimate of Zac's mass.

8 Razi has a scoop that can hold 200 g of flour.
He estimates that a sack of flour holds 50 times as much as his scoop does,
Work out an estimate of the mass of flour in a sack.
Give your answer in kilograms (kg).

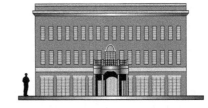

9 Sasha has a box that contains 12 standard cans of soda.
Estimate the mass of the full box of soda.
Give your answer in kilograms (kg).

10 The diagram shows a man standing next to a building.
  a Estimate the height of the building.
  b Estimate the length of the building
  Show how you worked out your answers.

Exercise 4.2 Kilometres and miles

1 Write down true (**T**) or false (**F**) for each of these statements.
  a 3 miles is further than 3 km.
  b 70 km is further than 70 miles.
  c 12.5 km is exactly the same distance as 12.5 miles.
  d 44 km is not as far as 44 miles.
  e In one hour, a person walking at 3 miles per hour will go a shorter distance than a person walking at 3 kilometres per hour.

2 Is Oditi correct?
  Explain your answer.

I have to travel 18 km to get to school.
My mother has to travel 18 miles to get to work.
I have to travel further to get to school than my mother has to travel to get to work.

3 Copy and complete these conversions of kilometres into miles.
  a 16 km $16 \div 8 = 2$ $2 \times 5 = \square$ miles
  b 32 km $32 \div 8 = \square$ $\square \times 5 = \square$ miles
  c 80 km $80 \div \square = \square$ $\square \times \square = \square$ miles

4 Convert the distances given in kilometres into miles.
  a 88 km   **b** 72 km   **c** 120 km   **d** 200 km

5 Copy and complete these conversions of miles into kilometres.
  a 15 miles $15 \div 5 = 3$ $3 \times 8 = \square$ km
  b 25 miles $25 \div 5 = \square$ $\square \times 8 = \square$ km
  c 55 miles $55 \div \square = \square$ $\square \times \square = \square$ km

6 Convert the distances given in miles into kilometres.
  a 30 miles   **b** 300 miles   **c** 45 miles   **d** 4500 miles

7 Which is further, 128 km or 75 miles?
  Show your working.

8 Which is further, 180 miles or 296 km?
  Show your working.

9 Use only numbers from the box to complete these statements.
  a 104 km = $\square$ miles
  b 95 miles = $\square$ km
  c $\square$ miles = $\square$ km
  d $\square$ km = $\square$ miles

168	105	190
304	65	152

10 Every car in the USA has a mileometer.
  The mileometer shows the <u>total distance</u> that a car has travelled.
  When Johannes bought a used car, the mileometer read:

  | 0 | 0 | 8 | 9 | 3 | 5 | miles

  Johannes paid $13 995 for the car.

  When Johannes wanted to sell the car, the mileometer read:

  | 0 | 4 | 5 | 4 | 0 | 5 | miles

  Johannes has been told that the value of his car will drop by about 5 cents for every kilometre he drives.
  How much money should Johannes expect to get for his car?

5 Angles

Exercise 5.1   Parallel lines

1 **a** State why *x* and *y* are equal.
    Copy the diagram.
    b Mark all the angles that are corresponding to *x*.
    c Mark all the angles that are alternate to *y*.

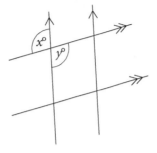

2 Find the values of *a*, *b*, *c* and *d*.
   Give a reason for each angle.

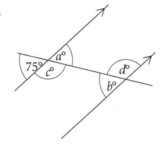

3 **a** Which angles are 68° because they are corresponding angles?
    b Which angles are 68° because they are alternate angles?

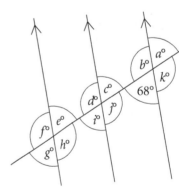

4 **a** Complete these sentences.
    i   Two alternate angles are ABG and … .
    ii   Another two alternate angles are CBE and … .
    iii Two corresponding angles are GEF and … .
   b Is Harsha correct?
    Explain your answer.

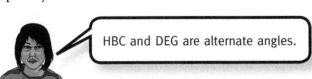

HBC and DEG are alternate angles.

5 Explain why only two of the lines *l*, *m* and *n* are parallel.

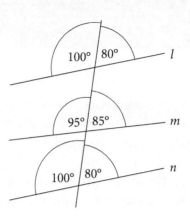

6 Give a reason why *t* must be 120°.

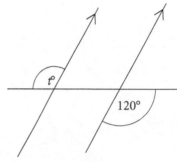

Not to scale

7 Are lines l_1 and l_2 parallel?
Give a reason for your answer.

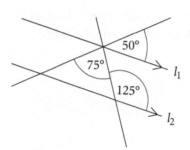

8 Explain why the sum of *a* and *b* must be 180°.

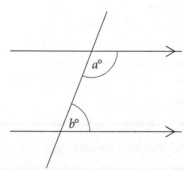

1   How big is each exterior angle of an equilateral triangle?

2   One of the exterior angles of an isosceles triangle is 30°.
    How big are the other two?

3   Use this diagram to show that the angle sum of triangle XYZ is 180°.

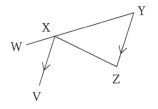

4   Here is an explanation that the angle sum of triangle ABC is 180°.
    The reasons for each line are missing.
    Give the reasons.
    1. Angle A of the triangle = angle PCA
    2. Angle B of the triangle = angle QCB
    3. Angle PCA + angle C of the triangle + angle QCB = 180°
    Hence angle A + angle B + angle C = 180°

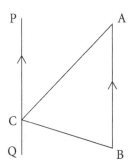

5   Show that the interior angles of this shape add up to 360°.

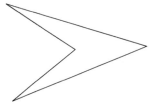

6   Use exterior angles to show that the angle sum of
    quadrilateral PQRS is 360°.

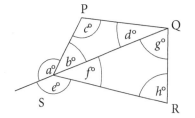

7   ABCD is a four-sided shape but two of the sides cross.
    a   Explain why the sum of the angles at A, B, C and
        D must be less than 360°.
    b   Find the sum of the angles at A, B, C and D,
        giving a reason for your answer.

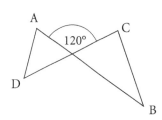

1 Explain why vertically opposite angles are equal.

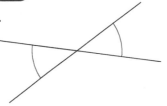

2 a Explain why $x + y + z = 360°$.

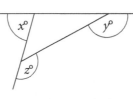

b Explain why $a + b + c + d = 360°$.

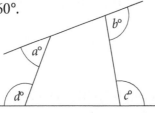

3 A, B, C and D are the four angles of a parallelogram.
a Show that angle A = angle C.
b Show that angle B = angle D.

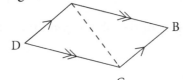

Use alternate angles.

4 Calculate the values of a, b and c.
Give reasons for your answers.

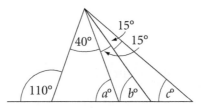

5 Calculate the values of x and y.
Give reasons for your answers.

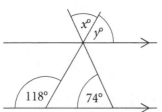

6 Show that the angles of this hexagon add up to 720°.

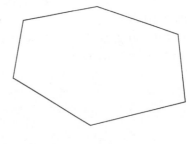

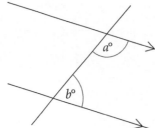

7 Explain why $a + b = 180°$.

6 Planning and collecting data

 Exercise 6.1   Collecting data

1 Which method of collection would you use to collect this data?

| Experiment | Observation | Survey |

a how often a slice of buttered bread lands 'butter down' when it is dropped 50 times
b the number of books owned by people living in your street or village
c the number of pairs of glasses owned by students in your class
d the number of people that go into your local dentist's surgery each hour
e how often a red card is drawn from a pack of playing cards in 50 draws
f the different makes of cars parked in your local grocery store car park
g how often students in your class have been to the cinema in the last month
h how often a normal dice lands on a 6 when it is rolled 50 times
i the number of students that ate fruit every day last week

2 A book club has 410 members.
The secretary of the club wants to know if the members would like a sudoku puzzle book to be included in the club magazine next month.
   a Give two reasons why the secretary should ask a sample of the members.
   b How many members of the book club should be in the sample?

3 Angela is an air hostess on a jumbo jet. She regularly does the air-safety briefing.
She wants to find out how many passengers have understood the air-safety briefing.
There are 394 passengers on the aeroplane.
Should Angela ask all the passengers on the aeroplane, or should she ask a sample?
Explain your answer.

4 There are 48 students in the fitness club at Maha's school.
Maha wants to know how many of these students brush their teeth at least twice a day.
She decides to ask a sample of the population.
   a Should Maha ask a sample of the population?
   b How many people should be in her survey?

5 There are 892 students in Dakarai's school.
Dakarai also wants to know how many students brush their
teeth at least twice a day.
He also decides to ask a sample of the population.
  a Should Dakarai ask a sample of the population?
  b How many people should be in his survey?

6 Edwardo sells books on the internet. He wants to work out the average price of the books he sells
each month. Should Edwardo use the population (all the books he sells) or a sample, in:
  a October, when he sells 37 books   **b** November, when he sells 55 books
  c December, when he sells 426 books   **d** January when he sells 20 books?
Give a reason for each of your answers. State the size of the sample, if appropriate.

7 Choose **A**, **B** or **C** as the most suitable degree of accuracy for
measuring each of these.

  a the time it takes students to walk around your school
    A nearest minute   **B** nearest second
    C nearest 0.1 of a second
  b the mass of a newborn kitten
    A nearest kilogram   **B** nearest 100 grams
    C nearest 1 gram
  c the width of students' hands in your class
    A nearest millimetre   **B** nearest centimetre
    C nearest metre
  d the time it takes a student to swim 1 km in a race
    A nearest hour   **B** nearest minute
    C nearest second

8 Hassan wants to know how many pairs of shoes the people in his village own.
He decides to carry out a survey. This is what he writes.

> The population of my village is 489, so I will interview a sample of 50 people.
> I will record their answers on the data collection sheet below.
>
> **Question**   How many pairs of shoes do you own?
> **Answer**
>
> | Number of pairs of shoes | 1-3 | 3-4 | 4-6 | 7-10 |
> |---|---|---|---|---|
> | Number of people | 3 5 6 | 2 3 8 15 | 5 7 11 17 21 | 3 4 7 8 |
>
> **Conclusion**   My results show that the people in my village don't have lots of
> pairs of shoes.

Think about the discussions you have had in class about questions like this.
Use your own and other people's ideas to answer these questions.
  a What do you think of Hassan's decision to ask a sample of 50 people?
  b What do you think of Hassan's data-collection sheet?
  c What do you think of Hassan's conclusion?
  d Design a better data-collection sheet for Hassan's question.

9 Xavier wants to know how often people in his village go to the cinema. He decides to carry out a survey. This is what he writes.

> *The population of my village is 118 people.*
> *I will interview a sample of 12 people, and record their answers on this data collection sheet.*
> *Question How often do you go to the cinema?*
> *Answer*
>
> | | Tally | Frequency |
> |---|---|---|
> | *Never* | I | *1* |
> | *Quite often* | IIII | *4* |
> | *Often* | IHT | *5* |
> | *Very often* | II | *2* |
>
> *Conclusion My results show me that the people in my village go to the cinema a lot.*

Think about the discussions you have had in class about questions like this.
Use your own and other people's ideas to answer these questions.
   a What do you think of Xavier's decision to ask a sample of 12 people?
   b What do you think of Xavier's data-collection sheet?
   c What do you think of Xavier's conclusion?
   d Design a better data-collection sheet for Xavier's question.

◆ Exercise 6.2   Types of data

1 Write down whether each set of data is discrete or continuous.
   a the number of trees in a garden
   b the number of flowers in a garden
   c the mass of fruit grown in a garden
   d the length of a bookshelf in a classroom
   e the number of desks in a classroom
   f the number of students with long hair
   g the time taken to complete a maths test
   h the number of marks in the maths test
   i the number of pizza slices on a plate
   j the weight of a slice of pizza

2 Read what Shen says.

> I have asked 10 people how tall they are, in centimetres. My results are 132, 144, 123, 155, 156, 175, 167, 150, 147 and 149. This is discrete data as the values are all whole numbers.

Is Shen correct?
Explain your answer.

3 Read what Tanesha says.

> I have weighed 10 small glass beads very accurately and rounded my answers to the nearest half a gram. My results are 6, $6\frac{1}{2}$, $6\frac{1}{2}$, 8, 9, $9\frac{1}{2}$, 10, 10, $10\frac{1}{2}$ and 11. This is continuous data as the values aren't whole numbers.

Is Tanesha correct?
Explain your answer.

Exercise 6.3 Using frequency tables

1 Write true (**T**) or false (**F**) for each statement.

   a $5 < 6$ **b** $5 \geq 6$ **c** $5 > 6$ **d** $5 \leq 6$

2 These are the lengths of 20 used pencils, measured to the nearest centimetre.

14	18	10	16	13
16	7	15	19	4
8	18	15	5	9
9	5	18	13	15

  a Copy and complete the grouped frequency table.

Length, l (cm)	Tally	Frequency
$1 < l \leq 5$		
$5 < l \leq 9$		
$9 < l \leq 13$		
$13 < l \leq 17$		
$17 < l \leq 21$		
Total		

  b How many of the pencils are more than 13 cm long but less than or equal to 17 cm long?

  c How many of the pencils are more than 9 cm long?
Explain how you use the grouped frequency table to work out your answer.

  d How many of the pencils are less than or equal to 13 cm long?
Explain how you use the grouped frequency table to work out your answer.

3 Here are the heights, in centimetres, of some sunflowers.

166	149	100	95	182	118	128	130	120
106	142	131	139	110	141	132	151	109

  a Put these heights into a grouped frequency table.
Use the class intervals $90 \leq h < 110$, $110 \leq h < 130$, $130 \leq h < 150$, $150 \leq h < 170$ and $170 \leq h < 190$.

  b How many sunflowers are there in the survey?

  c How many of the sunflowers are at least 150 cm high?

  d How many of the sunflowers are less than 130 cm high?

4 The two-way table shows the genders of a group of surfers on a beach and the type of clothes they were wearing.

	Swimwear	Wet suit	Other clothing	Total
Male	6	12	3	21
Female	2	7	0	9
Total	8	19	3	30

  a How many of the females were wearing wet suits?

  b How many of the surfers were wearing swimwear?

  c How many surfers were on the beach?

  d How many of the surfers were not wearing wet suits?

5 The two-way table shows some information about the breeds of horses at a horseshow.

	Arabian	Morgan	Thoroughbred	Other	Total
Female owner	42	18		4	119
Male owner	26		25		
Total		62			222

   a Copy and complete the table.
      Use the 'Total' column and the 'Total' row to help work out the missing values in the table.
   b How many of the Morgan horses have male owners?
   c How many of the horses were not Thoroughbred horses?

6 A factory manufactures 30 500 batteries an hour, of which 6500 are rechargeable.
It makes 3000 ordinary AAA batteries an hour.
Of the 10 000 AA batteries it makes an hour, 4000 are rechargeable.
The factory makes 15 000 ordinary and 1500 rechargeable C cell batteries an hour.
Copy and complete the two-way table to show the numbers of batteries made per hour.

	AAA	AA	C cell	Total
Ordinary				
Rechargeable				
Total				

7 A group of 30 friends went to the cinema.
They each bought one snack. They bought a chocolate bar, an ice cream or some popcorn.
Thirteen of the group bought a chocolate bar; only three of them were boys.
Four of the 16 girls bought popcorn. So did eight boys.
Copy and complete the two-way table to show the snacks bought by the group of friends.

	Chocolate bar	Ice cream	Popcorn	Total
Boys				
Girls				
Total				

7 Fractions

◆ **Exercise 7.1   Finding equivalent fractions, decimals and percentages**

1 Here is a list of commonly used fractions, decimals and percentages.

| 10%   90%   30% $\frac{2}{5}$ $\frac{3}{4}$ 0.5   0.8 $\frac{9}{10}$ 20% |

Use the numbers from the list to fill in the boxes. You can use each number only once.

a $\frac{3}{10} = \square$ **b** $0.4 = \square$ **c** $80\% = \square$ **d** $0.1 = \square$

e $\frac{1}{5} = \square$ **f** $75\% = \square$ **g** $\frac{1}{2} = \square$ **h** $\square = \square$

2 Write each percentage as: **i** a decimal   **ii** a fraction.
   a 99%   **b** 88%   **c** 16%   **d** 4%

3 Write each decimal as: **i** a percentage   **ii** a fraction.
   a 0.98   **b** 0.78   **c** 0.12   **d** 0.05

4 Write each fraction as: **i** a decimal   **ii** a percentage.
   a $\frac{9}{20}$ **b** $\frac{3}{50}$ **c** $\frac{17}{20}$ **d** $\frac{24}{25}$

5 By first changing the denominators to 10, 100 or 1000, write each fraction as:
   i a decimal   **ii** a percentage.
   a $\frac{3}{8}$ **b** $\frac{1}{40}$ **c** $\frac{16}{200}$ **d** $\frac{17}{125}$
   e $\frac{21}{40}$ **f** $\frac{8}{20}$ **g** $\frac{5}{8}$ **h** $\frac{301}{500}$

6 Here is part of Anders' homework.
   Anders has made a mistake. What is it?

> _Question_ Without using a calculator, work
> out $\frac{3}{40}$ as a percentage.
>
> _Answer_ $\frac{3}{40} = \frac{6}{80} = \frac{9}{120} = \frac{12}{160} = \frac{15}{200}$
>
> $\frac{15}{200} = \frac{150}{2000} = \frac{75}{1000} = 75\%$

Write down the correct answer, showing all of your working clearly.

1   Use division to convert each fraction to a terminating decimal.

   a $\frac{7}{8}$ b $\frac{7}{16}$ c $\frac{7}{20}$

   d $\frac{7}{25}$ e $\frac{7}{40}$ f $\frac{7}{80}$

2   Use division to convert each fraction to a recurring decimal.

   a $\frac{2}{9}$ b $\frac{2}{99}$ c $\frac{2}{999}$

   d $\frac{2}{11}$ e $\frac{2}{33}$ f $\frac{2}{66}$

3   Use division to convert each fraction to a decimal, correct to three decimal places.

   a $\frac{3}{7}$ b $\frac{3}{11}$ c $\frac{3}{13}$

   d $\frac{3}{14}$ e $\frac{3}{22}$ f $\frac{3}{26}$

 4   Read what Ahmad says.

> My teacher says that $\frac{1}{150} = 0.00\dot{6}$ and that $\frac{2}{150} = 0.01\dot{3}$.
> She must be wrong because $\frac{2}{150}$ is double $\frac{1}{150}$, but
> double 0.006 is 0.012 not 0.013.

Is Ahmad correct?
Explain your answer.

 5   Read what Zalika says.

> I worked out on my calculator that 2 ÷ 3 = 0.6666666667.
> This means that two thirds is not a recurring decimal as the
> sixes don't go on for ever: there's a seven on the end.

Do you think Zalika is correct?
Explain your answer.

◆ Exercise 7.3 Ordering fractions

1 This is part of Alicia's homework.

> <u>Question</u> Use equivalent fractions to write these fractions in order of
>
> size, smallest first: $\frac{1}{3}$ $\frac{2}{5}$ $\frac{4}{15}$
>
> <u>Answer</u> $3 \times 5 = 15$, so $\frac{1}{3 \times 5} = \frac{1}{15}$
>
> $5 + 10 = 15$, so $\frac{2+10}{5+10} = \frac{12}{15}$
>
> So the fractions are $\frac{1}{15}$, $\frac{12}{15}$, $\frac{4}{15}$
>
> In order of size the fractions are $\frac{1}{15}$, $\frac{4}{15}$, $\frac{12}{15}$
>
> which is the same as $\frac{1}{3}$, $\frac{4}{15}$, $\frac{2}{5}$

a Alicia has made several mistakes. What are they?
b Use equivalent fractions to write the fractions in order of size, <u>smallest</u> first.

2 Use equivalent fractions to write these fractions in order of size, <u>largest</u> first.

  a $\frac{3}{4}, \frac{1}{2}, \frac{3}{8}$ **b** $\frac{1}{4}, \frac{5}{12}, \frac{1}{6}$ **c** $\frac{3}{4}, \frac{5}{8}, \frac{11}{16}$

  d $\frac{1}{4}, \frac{2}{5}, \frac{3}{10}$ **e** $\frac{4}{5}, \frac{7}{10}, \frac{18}{25}$ **f** $\frac{1}{2}, \frac{2}{5}, \frac{3}{8}$

3 Use division to write these fractions in order of size, <u>smallest</u> first.

  a $\frac{1}{2}, \frac{2}{3}, \frac{3}{7}$ **b** $\frac{1}{3}, \frac{3}{10}, \frac{6}{19}$ **c** $\frac{5}{8}, \frac{13}{21}, \frac{19}{30}$

  d $\frac{5}{9}, \frac{7}{12}, \frac{11}{19}$ **e** $\frac{5}{6}, \frac{7}{9}, \frac{10}{13}$ **f** $\frac{23}{30}, \frac{31}{40}, \frac{67}{90}$

 4 Write these fractions in order of size, <u>smallest</u> first.
Show your working.

  $\frac{3}{4}, \frac{5}{8}, \frac{17}{24}, \frac{12}{17}$

 5 Mia arranges these fraction cards in order of size, <u>largest</u> first.
Without doing any calculations, explain how you can tell that Mia has arranged the
cards in the correct order.

  $\frac{1}{4}$ $\frac{1}{5}$ $\frac{1}{6}$ $\frac{1}{7}$ $\frac{1}{8}$

Exercise 7.4 Adding and subtracting fractions

1 Work out these additions and subtractions. Write each answer in its simplest form.

a $\frac{1}{2}+\frac{1}{4}$ b $\frac{1}{3}+\frac{1}{6}$ c $\frac{3}{4}+\frac{1}{12}$ d $\frac{3}{5}-\frac{7}{20}$ e $\frac{10}{21}-\frac{1}{7}$

2 Work out these additions and subtractions.
Write each answer in its simplest form. Write as a mixed number when appropriate.

a $\frac{1}{2}+\frac{4}{7}$ b $\frac{3}{4}-\frac{1}{6}$ c $\frac{7}{10}+\frac{7}{15}$ d $\frac{5}{8}-\frac{1}{6}$ e $\frac{3}{8}+\frac{11}{12}$

3 Copy and complete these additions.

a $3\frac{2}{5}+4\frac{1}{4}$ ① $3+4=7$ ② $\frac{2}{5}+\frac{1}{4}=\frac{\square}{20}+\frac{\square}{20}=\frac{\square}{20}$ ③ $7+\frac{\square}{20}=7\frac{\square}{20}$

b $5\frac{1}{4}+4\frac{5}{6}$ ① $5+4=9$ ② $\frac{1}{4}+\frac{5}{6}=\frac{\square}{12}+\frac{\square}{12}=\frac{\square}{12},\frac{\square}{12}=1\frac{\square}{12}$ ③ $9+1\frac{\square}{12}=10\frac{\square}{12}$

4 Copy and complete these subtractions.

a $7\frac{2}{3}-4\frac{1}{5}$ ① $\frac{23}{3}-\frac{21}{5}$ ② $\frac{23}{3}-\frac{21}{5}=\frac{\square}{15}-\frac{\square}{15}=\frac{\square}{15}$ ③ $\frac{\square}{15}=3\frac{\square}{15}$

b $8\frac{2}{5}-5\frac{9}{10}$ ① $\frac{42}{5}-\frac{\square}{10}$ ② $\frac{42}{5}-\frac{\square}{10}=\frac{\square}{10}-\frac{\square}{10}=\frac{\square}{10}$ ③ $\frac{\square}{10}=\frac{\square}{2}=\square\frac{\square}{2}$

5 Work out these additions and subtractions. Show all the steps in your working.

a $2\frac{2}{3}+\frac{5}{6}$ b $5\frac{5}{6}-\frac{11}{12}$ c $1\frac{1}{8}+1\frac{7}{24}$ d $4\frac{3}{4}-1\frac{15}{16}$ e $5\frac{5}{32}+1\frac{1}{8}$

f $10\frac{3}{10}-8\frac{4}{5}$ g $11\frac{1}{2}+3\frac{3}{5}$ h $6\frac{1}{4}-3\frac{5}{12}$ i $4\frac{2}{5}+2\frac{4}{11}$ j $8\frac{1}{8}-6\frac{1}{6}$

6 One of these cards gives a different answer to the other two.

A $2\frac{4}{9}+5\frac{5}{6}$ B $3\frac{5}{9}+4\frac{11}{18}$ C $4\frac{7}{9}+3\frac{1}{2}$

Which one is it? Show all your working.

7 One of these cards gives a different answer to the other two.

A $4\frac{19}{20}-2\frac{7}{10}$ B $5\frac{14}{15}-3\frac{3}{5}$ C $5\frac{4}{7}-3\frac{5}{21}$

Which one is it? Show all your working.

8 Bim and Yolander have both been out for a training run.

Bim ran for $8\frac{5}{8}$ kilometres.

Yolander ran for $10\frac{3}{4}$ kilometres.

a What is the difference between the distances run by Bim and Yolander?
b How far in total did Bim and Yolander run?

Exercise 7.5 Finding fractions of a quantity

1 Work these out mentally.

  a $\frac{1}{2}$ of \$15   **b** $\frac{3}{7}$ of 21 mm   **c** $\frac{5}{9}$ of 36 km

  d $\frac{3}{11}$ of 55 kg   **e** $\frac{5}{6}$ of 24 cm   **f** $\frac{2}{7}$ of 35 g

2 Work out these fractions of quantities. Give each answer as a mixed number.

  a $\frac{2}{3}$ of 10 cm   **b** $\frac{3}{4}$ of 31 ml   **c** $\frac{5}{6}$ of \$25

  d $\frac{4}{9}$ of 23 kg   **e** $\frac{3}{10}$ of 33 mm   **f** $\frac{3}{20}$ of 11 m

 3 One of these cards gives a different answer to the other two.

> **A** $\frac{7}{8}$ of 24   **B** $\frac{5}{7}$ of 28

> **C** $\frac{4}{5}$ of 25

  Which one is it? Show all your working.

 4 One of these cards gives a different answer to the other two.

> **A** $\frac{2}{3}$ of 28

> **B** $\frac{3}{4}$ of 25   **C** $\frac{1}{6}$ of 112

  Which one is it? Show all your working.

 5 Jake has nine cards. The nine cards represent three questions with their answers.
  Put the cards together to make the three questions with the correct answers.

> $\frac{4}{5}$ of 28 $= 19\frac{3}{5}$ $\frac{7}{10}$ of 27

> $= 19\frac{1}{5}$ $\frac{11}{15}$ of 24 $= 19\frac{4}{5}$

Exercise 7.6 Multiplying an integer by a fraction

1 Work these out mentally.

   a $\frac{1}{2} \times 50$ **b** $\frac{3}{4} \times 60$ **c** $\frac{5}{6} \times 30$

   d $\frac{5}{8} \times 32$ **e** $\frac{3}{10} \times 110$ **f** $\frac{1}{12} \times 120$

2 Work these out. Give each answer as a mixed number in its lowest terms.

   a $\frac{2}{3} \times 22$ **b** $\frac{4}{5} \times 16$ **c** $\frac{6}{7} \times 12$

   d $\frac{5}{9} \times 14$ **e** $\frac{4}{11} \times 23$ **f** $\frac{3}{13} \times 24$

3 Work these out. Give each answer as a mixed number in its lowest terms.
   Cancel before you do any calculations.

   a $\frac{3}{4} \times 18$ **b** $\frac{5}{6} \times 21$ **c** $\frac{5}{8} \times 22$

   d $\frac{5}{9} \times 24$ **e** $\frac{3}{10} \times 35$ **f** $\frac{7}{12} \times 33$

4 This is part of Oditi's homework.
   Has Oditi worked out the answer correctly?
   Explain your answer.

   Question Work out $\frac{5}{12} \times 68$.

   Answer $\frac{5}{\underset{4}{12}} \times 68^{17}, 5 \times 17 = 85, 85 \div 4 = 20\frac{5}{4}$

Exercise 7.7 Dividing an integer by a fraction

1 Work these out.

   a $14 \div \frac{1}{2}$ **b** $16 \div \frac{2}{3}$ **c** $18 \div \frac{3}{5}$ **d** $20 \div \frac{5}{7}$ **e** $22 \div \frac{11}{25}$ **f** $24 \div \frac{6}{7}$

2 Work these out. Give each answer as a mixed number in its lowest terms.
   In all parts, cancel before you do any calculations.

   a $22 \div \frac{4}{7}$ **b** $10 \div \frac{4}{5}$ **c** $21 \div \frac{14}{31}$ **d** $50 \div \frac{15}{17}$ **e** $32 \div \frac{24}{25}$ **f** $18 \div \frac{8}{11}$

3 One of these cards gives a different answer from the other two.

   | **A** $14 \div \frac{2}{7}$ | **B** $20 \div \frac{5}{12}$ | **C** $26 \div \frac{13}{24}$ |

   Which one is it? Show all your working.

Exercise 7.8 Multiplying and dividing fractions

1 Work these out mentally.

  a $\frac{1}{4} \times \frac{1}{3}$ **b** $\frac{3}{4} \times \frac{3}{4}$ **c** $\frac{5}{7} \times \frac{1}{6}$

  d $\frac{3}{4} \times \frac{3}{5}$ **e** $\frac{3}{5} \times \frac{2}{7}$ **f** $\frac{5}{8} \times \frac{2}{3}$

2 Work these out mentally. Cancel each answer to its simplest form.

  a $\frac{4}{5} \times \frac{1}{2}$ **b** $\frac{2}{3} \times \frac{3}{5}$ **c** $\frac{3}{4} \times \frac{2}{5}$

  d $\frac{3}{4} \times \frac{2}{3}$ **e** $\frac{7}{8} \times \frac{8}{11}$ **f** $\frac{5}{9} \times \frac{18}{25}$

3 Work these out mentally.

  a $\frac{1}{2} \div \frac{2}{3}$ **b** $\frac{1}{4} \div \frac{3}{5}$ **c** $\frac{3}{7} \div \frac{1}{2}$

  d $\frac{5}{9} \div \frac{6}{7}$ **e** $\frac{2}{5} \div \frac{5}{9}$ **f** $\frac{1}{10} \div \frac{3}{7}$

4 Work these out mentally. Write each answer as a mixed number.

  a $\frac{1}{2} \div \frac{1}{3}$ **b** $\frac{3}{5} \div \frac{4}{7}$ **c** $\frac{1}{3} \div \frac{2}{7}$

  d $\frac{7}{9} \div \frac{1}{2}$ **e** $\frac{5}{6} \div \frac{2}{11}$ **f** $\frac{4}{7} \div \frac{3}{13}$

5 Work these out mentally. Cancel each answer to its simplest form.

  a $\frac{5}{8} \div \frac{1}{2}$ **b** $\frac{4}{13} \div \frac{3}{13}$ **c** $\frac{5}{8} \div \frac{5}{12}$

  d $\frac{1}{3} \div \frac{5}{9}$ **e** $\frac{1}{4} \div \frac{1}{12}$ **f** $\frac{7}{9} \div \frac{1}{6}$

 6 Anders and Alicia have been asked to work out $\frac{1}{2} \times \frac{2}{3} \times \frac{3}{4} \times \frac{4}{5} \times \frac{5}{6} \times \frac{6}{7}$ mentally.

That's impossible! I can't do such a huge multiplication in my head!

It's quite easy really. You just have to do lots of cancelling first.

  a What fraction would Anders get if he multiplied all the numbers without cancelling?
  b What fraction would Alicia get if she cancelled first and then multiplied? Show your working.

8 Shapes and geometric reasoning

◆ Exercise 8.1   Recognising congruent shapes

1 Which side is the hypotenuse in each right-angled triangle?

a 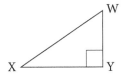   **b** 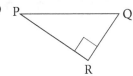   **c**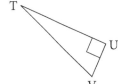

2 Read what Maha says.

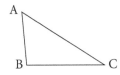

> AC looks like the hypotenuse of triangle ABC, but AC is not a hypotenuse at all.

Explain why Maha is correct.

3 Which of the following shapes are congruent to shape A?

A   B   C   D   E   F   G

4 These two triangles are congruent.

   a Write down the length of: **i** AC   **ii** QR   **iii** BC.
   b Write down the size of: **i** ∠BAC   **ii** ∠RPQ   **iii** ∠PQR.

 5 These quadrilaterals are congruent.

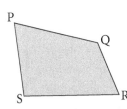   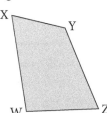

   a Write down the side that corresponds to: **i** SR   **ii** QR   **iii** YZ   **iv** WZ.
   b Write down the angle that corresponds to: **i** ∠PQR   **ii** ∠QRS   **iii** ∠XWZ   **iv** ∠WZY.

Exercise 8.2   Identifying symmetry of 2D shapes

1 Copy each of these shapes. On your copies, draw the lines of symmetry.

a   b   c   d

e   f 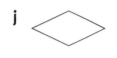 g   h

i   j   k   l

2 For each of the shapes in question **1**, write down the order of rotational symmetry.

3 Write down the number of lines of symmetry for each of these shapes.

a   b   c   d

e   f g h

4 For each of the shapes in question **3**, write down the order of rotational symmetry.

5 In each diagram the dotted lines are lines of symmetry but some grey squares are missing. Copy and complete each diagram.

a 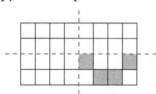   b 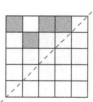   c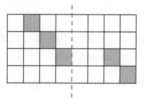

 6 Anders has made this pattern from grey and black tiles.

> There are six different ways I can add the two black tiles to the pattern to make a pattern with only one line of symmetry. There is only one way I can add the two black tiles to the pattern to make a pattern with two lines of symmetry.

He has two spare black tiles.
Show that Anders is correct.
You can only join the tiles side-to-side like this ▢▢ , not corner to corner like this 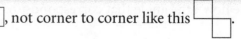 .

♦ **Exercise 8.3 Classifying quadrilaterals**

1 Write down the name of each special quadrilateral that is described.
   a All my sides are the same length.
       My diagonals bisect each other at 90°.
       I have order 2 rotational symmetry.
   b My diagonals cross at 90°, but I have no parallel sides.
   c I have four corners, all of them are 90°.
       My diagonals bisect each other, but not at 90°.

2 Put each quadrilateral through this classification flow chart.
   Write down the number where each shape comes out.
   a square   **b** rhombus   **c** rectangle   **d** parallelogram
   e trapezium   **f** isosceles trapezium   **g** kite

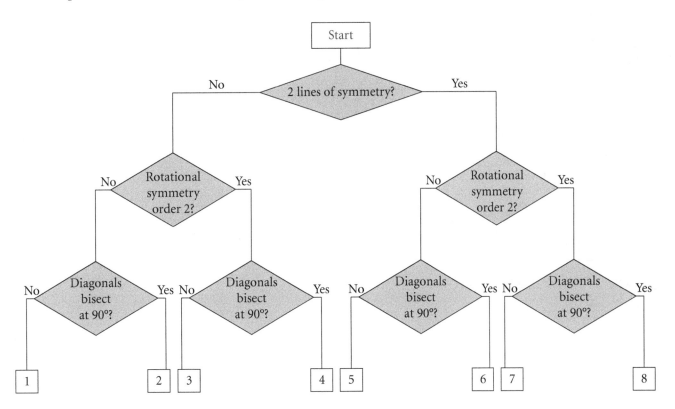

3 Plot these points on a coordinate grid.
   A(1, 1), B(1, 2), C(1, 4), D(1, 6), E(2, 4), F(3, 2), G(3, 6), H(5, 4), I(4, 4), J(5, 1), K(7, 6)
   Write down the coordinates of the point where the diagonals cross in each quadrilateral.
   a BDGF   **b** AEIJ   **c** CGKH

1 Sketch a net for each cuboid.

a 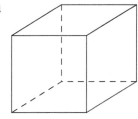   **b**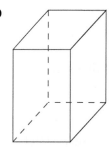

2 Which of these could be the net of a cuboid?

A

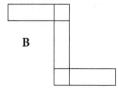
B

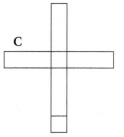
C

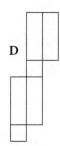
D

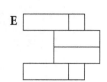
E

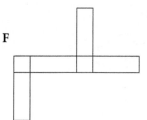
F

3 Sketch a net for this triangular-based pyramid.

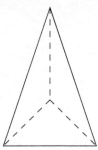

4 Draw an accurate net for each of these 3D solids.

a cuboid

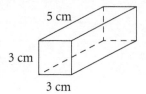

b triangular prism (right-angled triangle)

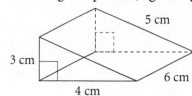

5 Here is the net of a cuboid.

When the net is folded to make the cuboid, side N meets side I. Which side meets:
a side C   **b** side E   **c** side G   **d** side A?

6 Dakarai has a cube with sides 6 cm long.
He labels the vertices (corners) A, B, C, D, E, F, G and H, as shown.

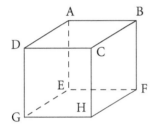

He draws a line from A to G to C to A.

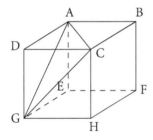

a Draw an accurate net of Dakarai's cuboid.
b Measure the total length of the line that Dakarai draws.
Give your answer to the nearest millimetre.

◆ Exercise 8.5   Making scale drawings

1 Oditi makes a scale drawing of the front of a large building.
She uses a scale of '1 cm represents 5 m'.
a On her drawing, the building is 16 cm long. How long is the building in real life?
b The building in real life is 120 m high. How high is the building on the scale drawing?

2 Harsha makes a scale drawing of a window.
She uses a scale of '1 cm represents 20 cm'.
   a On her drawing the window is 6 cm wide. How wide is the window in real life?
   Give your answer in metres.
   b The window in real life is 2.2 m high. How high is the window on the scale drawing?
   Give your answer in centimetres.

3 Hassan makes a scale drawing of his garden.
He uses centimetre-squared paper. He uses a scale of 1 to 200.

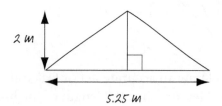

(Grid diagram with points A, B, C, D, E, F forming an L-shaped garden)

   a Calculate the distance in real life of each of
   these lengths. Give your answers in metres.
     i AB   **ii** BC   **iii** CD
     iv DE   **v** EF   **iv** AF
   b The path in Hassan's garden is 11 m long.
   How long will it be on the scale drawing?
   Give your answers in centimetres.
   c The flowerbed in Hassan's garden is 3 m wide.
   How wide will it be on the scale drawing?
   Give your answer in centimetres.

4 This is a sketch of part of a roof.
   a Make a scale drawing of this roof section.
   Use a scale of 1 : 25.
   b What is the real-life length of the hypotenuse of the roof?
   Give your answer in metres, to the nearest centimetre.

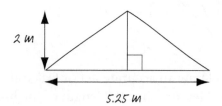

2 m

5.25 m

5 A rectangular football pitch is 100 m long and 70 m wide.
What is the length of a diagonal of the football pitch?
Explain how you worked out your answer.
Show all your working.

6 This is a sketch of Shen's bedroom.
   a Make an scale drawing of his bedroom.
   Use a scale of 1 to 50.
   b What is the real-life length of the dotted line AB?
   Give your answer in metres.

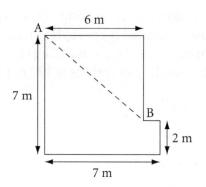

6 m

A

7 m

B

2 m

7 m

9 Simplifying expressions and solving equations

◆ **Exercise 9.1   Collecting like terms**

1 Rewrite these expressions. Follow the guidelines in the Coursebook.
   a $7 + 3a + 5a$ **b** $8 + b$ **c** $c3$ **d** $y5d$
   e $6x + 11e$ **f** $-3 + 5f$ **g** $10 + 3 \times g$ **h** $h \times w \times 3$
   i $4 \times v + i8$ **j** $-2j + 5 \times u$ **k** $-9tk + 3$ **l** $-3sl - 4rq$

2 Jake has this set of cards.

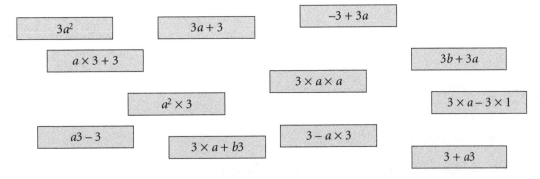

   a Put the cards into groups of expressions that have the same meaning.
   b **i** Write down the expression on the card that is left over.
      ii Rewrite the expression on this card using the guidelines in the Coursebook.

3 Simplify each expression.
   a $7a + a + 3a$ **b** $3b - 5b + 4b$ **c** $3c - c - 4c$ **d** $9d + 5e - 6d - 4e$
   e $7f - 5g - 5f + g$ **f** $5ef + 5ef - 3fe$ **g** $5gh + 6ba + 7gh - 8ab$ **h** $3h + 12 - 3 - 2h$
   i $6i - 4j - 9j + 8i$ **j** $4j + 8j + 7j^2 - 2j^2$ **k** $8k^2 - 2k - 3k^2$ **l** $6l + 3l^2 + 6 - l^2 - 6l$

4 Copy and complete this algebraic pyramid.

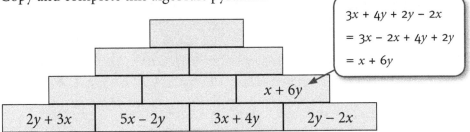

$3x + 4y + 2y - 2x$
$= 3x - 2x + 4y + 2y$
$= x + 6y$

Remember that in an algebraic pyramid you find the expression in each block by <u>adding</u> the expressions in the two blocks <u>below</u> it.

$x + 6y$

| $2y + 3x$ | $5x - 2y$ | $3x + 4y$ | $2y - 2x$ |

5 Copy and complete this algebraic pyramid.

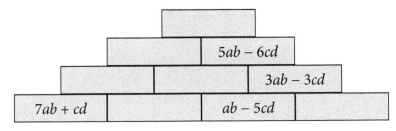

6 Make two copies of the algebraic pyramid below. Complete both of your pyramids.

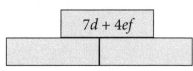

$$7d + 4ef$$

For questions **6** and **7** there are <u>lots</u> of different answers. You need to work out two of them for each question.

7 Make two copies of the algebraic pyramid below. Complete both of your pyramids.

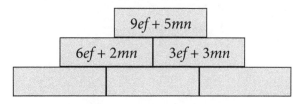

$$9ef + 5mn$$
$$6ef + 2mn \qquad 3ef + 3mn$$

8 This is part of Hassan's homework.

> _Question_ _Simplify each expression._
>
> 1. $11xy - xy + 5xz$
> 2. $5a^2 + 4cb - 3a^2 - bc$
>
> _Answer_   1. $11xy - xy + 5xz = 10xy + 5xz = 15xyz$
> 2. $5a^2 + 4cb - 3a^2 - bc = 2a^2 + 4cb - bc$

He has made several mistakes.
a Explain what he has done wrong.
b Work out the correct answers.

◆ Exercise 9.2   Expanding brackets

1 Expand the brackets. Follow the conventions for writing algebraic expressions.
   a $6(a + 6)$ **b** $5(b + 7)$ **c** $7(c - 8)$ **d** $6(d - 9)$ **e** $5(8 + e)$
   f $7(7 + f)$ **g** $6(6 - g)$ **h** $5(7 - h)$ **i** $7(8i + 9)$ **j** $6(8 + 7j)$
   k $5(6k - 7)$ **l** $7(8 - 9l)$ **m** $6(9a + 8m)$ **n** $5(7b + 6n)$ **o** $7(7c - 8x)$
   p $6(9px + 8y)$ **q** $5(7qy - 6x)$ **r** $7(7r + s + 8)$ **s** $3(a - 3b - 1)$ **t** $5(x - y - z)$

2 Read what Jake says.

> If I expand $4(a - 7)$ and $4(7 - a)$ I will get the same answer, as both expressions have exactly the same terms in them.

Is Jake correct?
Explain your answer.

3 Expand and simplify each expression.
   a $6(a + 7) + 8(a + 9)$ **b** $8(b + 7) + 6(5b + 6)$ **c** $7(c + 8) + 9(8 + 7c)$
   d $7(8d + 9) - 8(d + 7)$ **e** $6(5 + 6e) - 7(8e + 9)$ **f** $9(8f + 7g) - 6(5g - 6f)$

4 Expand each expression.

a $a(a + 1)$ **b** $b(b - 5)$ **c** $c(3c + 6)$
d $d(3x - 3)$ **e** $e(3e + 6)$ **f** $f(1 + 5f)$
g $g(7 - 3x)$ **h** $h(6 - x)$ **i** $i(3i + 7x)$
j $j(3a - 7j)$ **k** $k(3k - 6x)$ **l** $l(3x - 6z)$
m $3m(m + 3x)$ **n** $3n(6n - 6)$ **o** $4x(6x - 3y)$
p $6p(3 + 3p)$ **q** $6q(6x + 5q)$ **r** $3r(3r - x - 3)$
s $2a(3 + 2a + b)$ **t** $3x(-z - y - x)$

5 Expand and simplify each expression.

a $a(a + 3) + a(a + 4)$ **b** $b(b + 3) + b(4b + 5)$
c $c(3c + 4) + c(5c + 6)$ **d** $d(3d + 4) - d(d + 5)$
e $e(3 + 4e) - e(5e - 6)$ **f** $f(3f + 4g) - 5f(6f - 7g)$

6 This is part of Razi's homework.
He has made a mistake in every question.

> _Question_ Expand and simplify each expression.
>
> 1. $3(a + 5) - 5(3a + 5)$
>
> 2. $p(4q + r) + q(2r - 4p)$
>
> 3. $5b(b + 3a) + a(4a + 6b)$
>
> _Answer_ 1. $3(a + 5) - 3(3a + 5) = 3a + 15 - 9a - 15$
> $$= 6a + 30$$
>
> 2. $p(4q + r) + q(2r - 4p) = 4pq + pr + 2qr - 4pq$
> $$= 3pr + pq$$
> $$= 4p^2qr$$
>
> 3. $5b(b + 3a) + a(4a + 6b) = 5b^2 + 15ab + 5ab + 4a^2 + 6ab$
> $$= 4a^2 + 5b^2 + 11ab$$

a Explain what he has done wrong.
b Work out the correct answers.

7 Read what Mia says.

> When I expand and simplify $x(x - 3) + x(x + 5)$, I get the same answer as when I expand $2x(x + 1)$.

Is Mia correct?
Explain your answer.

◆ Exercise 9.3 Constructing and solving equations

1 Work out the value of the algebraic unknown in each diagram.
All measurements are in centimetres.

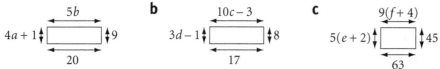

a

$4a + 1$ | $5b$ | 9
20

b

$3d - 1$ | $10c - 3$ | 8
17

c

$5(e + 2)$ | $9(f + 4)$ | 45
63

> Remember that the algebraic unknown is a letter that represents a number.

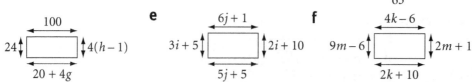

d

100
24 | | $4(h - 1)$
$20 + 4g$

e

$6j + 1$
$3i + 5$ | | $2i + 10$
$5j + 5$

f

$4k - 6$
$9m - 6$ | | $2m + 1$
$2k + 10$

2 Work out the value of the algebraic unknown in each of these isosceles triangles.
All measurements are in centimetres.

a $3a - 4$ 20

b 21 $3(b + 2)$

c $c + 18$ 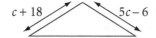 $5c - 6$ **d** $2(d + 1)$  $d + 10$

3 Work out the value of x in each isosceles trapezium.
All measurements are in centimetres.

a $7(x - 2)$ $3x + 6$ **b** $3x + 6$ $6(x - 1)$

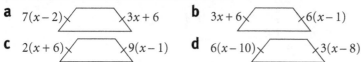

c $2(x + 6)$ $9(x - 1)$ **d** $6(x - 10)$ $3(x - 8)$

4 For each part of this question:
i write down an equation to represent the problem
ii compare the equation you have written with the equations written by the other members of your group
iii decide who has written the correct equation in the easiest way
iv solve the equation that you chose in part **iii**.

a Xavier thinks of a number. He multiplies it by 2 then adds 8. The answer is 20.
What number did Xavier think of?

b Sasha thinks of a number. She divides it by 4 then subtracts 3. The answer is 2.
What number did Sasha think of?

c Harsha thinks of a number. She multiplies it by 4 then subtracts 6. The answer is the same as 2 times the number plus 12.
What number did Harsha think of?

d Anders thinks of a number. He multiplies it by 5 then adds 10. The answer is the same as 7 times the number.
What number did Anders think of?

e Ahmad thinks of a number. He adds 1 then multiplies the result by 3. The answer is the same as 4 times the number take away 4.
What number did Ahmad think of?

f Zalika thinks of a number. She subtracts 6 then multiplies the result by 5. The answer is the same as subtracting 5 from the number then multiplying by 4.
What number did Zalika think of?

10 Processing and presenting data

◆ Exercise 10.1 Calculating statistics from discrete data

1 These are the numbers of goals scored in 20 football matches.
Find:
  a the mode
  b the median
  c the mean number of goals scored.

0	2	6	4	3
1	3	4	4	4
1	0	5	0	2
4	0	2	4	3

2 This table shows the numbers of matches in 60 matchboxes.

Number of matches	47	48	49	50	51	52	53	54
Number of boxes	3	5	8	11	14	9	7	3

  a Find:
    i the mode   **ii** the median   **iii** the mean   **iv** the range of the numbers.
  b It says on the box: 'Average contents 50 matches'. Is this correct?
     Give a reason for your answer.

3 These are the ages of 50 children in a small school.

Age	6	7	8	9	10	11
Frequency	12	9	8	10	8	3

  a Find: **i** the mode   **ii** the median
          iii the mean   **iv** the range of the ages.
  b What will the median age of these children be in five years' time?
  c What will the mean age of these children be in five years' time?
  d What will the range of the ages of these children be in five years' time?

4 Some children in a swimming club recorded how many lengths they could swim without stopping. Here are the results.

Lengths	0	1	2	3	4
Number of children	4	11	8	6	3

  a How many children swam more than the modal number of lengths?
  b How many children swam more than the median number?
  c Work out the mean.

5 A group of 30 children recorded how many brothers and sisters they had. This table shows the results.
Find: **a** the mode   **b** the median
     c the mean number of brothers and sisters.

Number of brothers and sisters	0	1	2	3	4	5
Frequency	2	8	8	8	1	3

6 The table shows the lengths of lessons per day, in some schools.

Length of lesson (minutes)	35	40	45	50	55	60
Number of schools	2	4	6	5	0	3

  a Find: **i** the range
          ii the mode
          iii the median
          iv the mean length of each lesson.
  b One school is thinking of changing the length of its lessons.
     Which would be the most useful average for it to know? Why?
  c Two of the schools increase the length of their lessons from 35 minutes to 45 minutes. Find the
     new value of: **i** the range   **ii** the mode   **iii** the median   **iv** the mean lesson length.

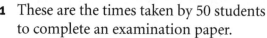

1 These are the times taken by 50 students to complete an examination paper.

Time (minutes)	20–	25–	30–	35–	40–45
Number of students	18	10	10	8	4

   a Write down the modal class.
   b Which class contains the median?
   c Estimate the mean.
   d Explain why the range must be less than 30 minutes.

> Remember that 20– means all values that are 20 or more, but less than 25.

2 This table shows the masses, to the nearest kilogram, of 30 parcels delivered by a driver.

Mass (kg)	5–7	8–10	11–13	14–16	17–19	20–22
Frequency	4	8	4	4	8	2

   a What is the modal class?
   b Estimate:
     i the median   **ii** the mean   **iii** the range of the masses.

3 Some children were throwing a tennis ball as far as they could. Here are the results.

Distance (m)	10–	14–	18–	22–	26–30
Number of children	3	14	9	4	2

   a What is the modal class?
   b Estimate:
     i the median   **ii** the mean   **iii** the range of the throwing distances.

4 This table shows how long 50 customers had to wait on a telephone helpline. The company says: 'The average waiting time is less than five minutes.' Show that this is not correct.

Time (minutes)	0–	2–	4–	6–	8–	10–	12–14
Frequency	2	10	12	10	7	5	4

5 This graph shows the attendance record for 50 students.
   a Write down the modal class.
   b Estimate the average percentage attendance.

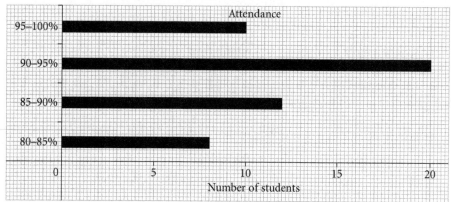

6 150 children guess the number of sweets in a jar.
They know there are fewer than 100.
This table lists their guesses.

Guess	50–59	60–69	70–79	80–89	90–99
Number of children	20	45	40	35	10

Estimate: **a** the range   **b** the median   **c** the mean of the guesses.

1 Here is some information about the ages of the men and women working in a company.
Describe the differences between the ages of the men and women.

> Refer to the average age and the range of the ages.

	Men	Women
Number of employees	43	72
Median age	38	29
Mean age	39.1	30.8
Modal age class	36–45	26–35
Youngest person	16	18
Oldest person	64	52

2 There were 10 rehearsals for a school musical. This table shows how many rehearsals the cast attended.

	Fewer than 6	6	7	8	9	10
Girls	0	0	0	5	8	12
Boys	0	2	3	5	4	6

Use an average and the range to compare the number of rehearsals attended by girls and boys.

 3 The table shows the number of goals scored in each match in the Men's Football World Cup in 2010 and the Women's Football World Cup in 2011.

Goals scored		0	1	2	3	4	5	6	7
World Cup	**Men 2010**	7	17	13	14	7	5	0	1
	Women 2011	1	8	4	9	8	1	1	0

a Which average is the best one to use to compare the goals scored by men's teams and women's teams?

b Use the average you have selected to decide whether more goals were scored in men's matches or women's matches.

 4 A group of students take a practice test. Here are the results.
Mean mark: 41.2 Range: 18 marks
After further teaching they take the real test. Their marks are recorded in this table.

Mark	36–40	41–45	46–50	51–55	55–60	61–65
Frequency	3	10	15	10	18	14

How did the mean and the range change from the practice test to the real test?

5 Some seeds were give fertiliser and others were not. This table shows the heights of the plants that grew from the seeds.

Height of plant (cm)		11–15	16–20	21–25	26–30	31–35	36–40	41–45
Frequency	**Without fertiliser**	4	5	7	2	2	0	0
	With fertiliser	1	3	6	4	8	2	1

a How did the fertiliser affect the range of heights?
b How did the fertiliser change the mean height?

11 Percentages

◆ **Exercise 11.1   Calculating percentages**

1 **a** Look at the box. Write each percentage as a decimal.
   b Write each percentage as a fraction in its simplest possible form.

30%	8%
12.5%	180%

2 Find each amount without using a calculator.
   a 75% of 28 metres   **b** 30% of 400 people   **c** $66\frac{2}{3}$% of 96 kg   **d** 5% of 2000

3 Use a calculator to work out these percentages.
   a 19% of 69   **b** 83% of 4300   **c** 6.5% of $286   **d** 14% of $2600

4 Work out these amounts. Do not use a calculator unless you need to.
   a 40% of 40 kg   **b** 39% of 39   **c** 70% of $210   **d** 12.5% of 80

5 42% of a number is 64.26.
   All the percentages in the table refer to the same number.
   Use the information given above to work out the missing numbers.

10.5%	21%	42%	63%	84%
		64.26		

6 The table shows the results of a survey of people's heights.

Height (m)	Less than 1.50	Between 1.50 and 1.80	More than 1.80
Percentage (%)	13	64	23

Altogether, 652 people took part (participated) in the survey.
Find the number of people in each height class.

7 Fill in the missing numbers.
   a 50% of 24 = 25% of …
   b 20% of 60 = 10% of …
   c 25% of 48 = 75% of …

8 There are 1225 students at a university college.
   43% are studying science or engineering. 7% own a car. 82% say it is a good college.
   How many students is that in each case?

9 The population of India is about 1200 million. This table shows how many people follow some
   different religions in India.

Religion	Hindu	Muslim	Sikh	Other
Percentage (%)	83	11	2	4

Work out the numbers of Hindus, Muslims and Sikhs in India.

10 Who had a better score, Sasha or Razi?
   Give a reason for your answer.

I scored 48 out of 65.   I scored 69%.

Exercise 11.2 Percentage increases and decreases

1 **a** Find 12% of 30.
   b Increase 30 kg by 12%.
   c Decrease 30 cm by 12%.

2 **a** Find 95% of 2000.
   b Increase 2000 people by 95%.
   c Decrease 2000 hours by 95%.

3 The price of a car is $4600. The price is reduced by 15%.
   a What is the price reduction?   **b** Find the new price of the car.

4 A town has 8400 inhabitants.
   a 15% of the inhabitants are at school. How many are at school?
   b 74% of the inhabitants are under 60. How many are under 60?
   c A new housing development increases the population of the town by 4%.
      What will be the new population?

5 This label is on a bag of dried fruit.
   The usual mass is 500 grams.
   What is the mass if an extra 25% is added?

   > 25% extra free!

6 Arthur finds that the values of some of his antiques have changed.

	Item	Original value ($)	Change in value
a	Painting	550	increase of 40%
b	Vase	395	decrease of 30%
c	Clock	1175	increase of 80%
d	Chair	745	decrease of 5%

Find the new value of each item.

7 Here are the prices, in dollars, of entry to an amusement park.

Adult	Child	Student	Family of four
17.90	9.70	15.40	49.50

The owners want to put up (raise) the prices by about 15%.
What should the new prices be? Round them to the nearest ten cents.

8 The River Indus is about 3200 km long.
   a The Mississippi is about 19% longer than the Indus.
      How long is the Mississippi?
   b The Rhine is about 62% shorter than the Indus. How long is the Rhine?

9 An electrical store has reduced some prices in a sale.

Item	DVDs	Computer games	Monitors
Original price ($)	12	40	190
Reduction	20%	15%	60%

Work out the new prices.

1 Change these test marks to percentages.
   a 29 out of 40   **b** 29 out of 50   **c** 57 out of 75   **d** 57 out of 80

2 Dolores organised a charity run. Altogether, 170 men, 220 women and 110 children took part.
Calculate the percentage of men, women and children.

3 There are 60 red pens and 20 blue pens in a box.
   a Find the percentages of red pens and blue pens.
   10 pens of each colour are removed from the box.
   b Find the new percentages of red pens and blue pens.

4 A shop sells large and small bags of rice.
On Monday 57 large bags and 132 small bags were sold.
   a What percentage of the bags sold were large?
   b What percentage of the bags sold were small?
   On Tuesday 73 large bags and 81 small bags were sold.
   c What percentage of the bags sold on the two days combined was large?

5 Find the percentage change in each case.
   a an increase from 50 to 70   **b** an increase from 250 to 277
   c an increase from 350 to 650   **d** an increase from 4000 to 4100
   e a decrease from 400 to 320   **f** a decrease from 300 to 30

6 A man wanted to reduce his mass by 10%. His mass was 109.5 kg.
After going on a diet he reduced his mass to 99.4 kg.
Has he achieved his goal? Give a reason for your answer.

7 A factory produces 40 cars per week.
What is the percentage change in the production rate if it changes to:
   a 30 cars per week   **b** 50 cars per week   **c** 75 cars per week
   d 80 cars per week   **e** 100 cars per week?

8 These are the usual times it takes Jason to make three car journeys.
First: 5 hours   Second: $2\frac{1}{2}$ hours   Third: $3\frac{1}{4}$ hours
Road repairs increase the time for each journey by 30 minutes.
Find the percentage increase in each journey time.

9 Caroline has a job. She works 38 hours a week and is paid $24 per hour.
She reduces her hours to 35 hours but her pay increases to $26 per hour.
Work out:
   a the percentage change in the hours she works
   b the percentage change in her hourly rate of pay
   c the percentage change in her total weekly pay.

10 a What percentage of 50 is 40?
   b What percentage of 40 is 50?
   c What percentage of 437 is 372?
   d What percentage of 372 is 437?

1

$$\frac{48}{59} \quad \frac{127}{161} \quad \frac{17}{21}$$

Write the fractions as percentages.

a Which fraction is the largest?
b Which fraction is the smallest?

2 Here are the results for two basketball teams.

	Wins	Games played
Highballs	20	32
Spikers	14	20

a Work out the percentage of wins for each team.
b Which team has the better record of wins?

3 The countries with the highest numbers of medals in the 2012 Olympic Games are listed in the table.

Medals won	Gold	Silver	Bronze
USA	46	29	29
China	38	27	23
GB	29	17	19

a Which country won the most medals?
b For each country, work out the percentage of their medals that were gold.
c Which country won the largest proportion of gold medals?

4 A biologist was testing two types of seeds.
He counted how many germinated. The results are shown in the table.
a What percentage of each type germinated?
b Which seeds had the better rate of germination?

	Number of seeds	
	Planted	Germinated
Type A	50	42
Type B	80	56

5 This table shows the numbers of televisions sold by two stores in two different weeks.
The first week was before a sale. The second week was during a sale.
a Work out the percentage increase in sales for each store during the sales week.
b Which store had a better increase in sales?

	Sales of TVs	
	Before the sale	During the sale
Store X	40	65
Store Y	90	116

6 Two classes did a timed run. After some training they did the run again. Here are the average times.
Which class had a better percentage decrease in times? Use percentages to justify your answer.

	Average time for the class (seconds)	
	Before training	After training
Class A	73.2	61.4
Class B	56.8	48.2

12 Constructions

Exercise 12.1 Drawing circles and arcs

1 Draw a circle with:

   a radius 5 cm   **b** radius 37 mm   **c** diameter 12 cm   **d** diameter 80 mm.

2 The diagram shows a horizontal line AB, which is 12 cm long.

A ————————————————————————————————————— B
        6 cm   X   each gap = 0.5 cm

   a Make an accurate copy of the diagram, leave out the letters and arrows.

   b Draw on your diagram circles with:

     i radius 6 cm, centred on the mark labelled X

     ii radius 5.5 cm, centred on the next mark

     iii radius 5 cm, centred on the next mark

     iv radius 4.5 cm, centred on the next mark

     v radius 4 cm, centred on the next mark.

   Continue with this pattern until you have drawn a circle with radius 0.5 cm.

   c Turn your diagram 90° anticlockwise. What 3D shape does it look like?

3 Draw an arc with:

   a radius 6 cm and angle 60°   **b** radius 6 cm and angle 135°.

4 Draw a horizontal line AB, 9 cm long.

   Open your compasses to a radius of 7 cm.

   Centre your compasses at each end of AB, in turn.

   Draw two large arcs that cross each other in two places.

   Label these points C and D.

   Use a straight-edge to draw straight lines from C to A and D to A.

   Your diagram should look like this:

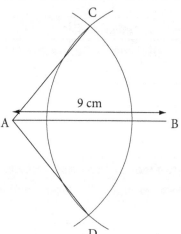

   Use a protractor to measure the size of angle CAD.

1 Follow these instructions to draw the perpendicular bisector of a line segment AB.

  a Draw a line segment 6 cm long. Label one end A and the other end B.
     Make sure you allow at least 5 cm of space above and below the line for drawing the arcs.

  b Open your compasses to a radius of 4 cm.

  c Put the point of the compasses on the end of the line marked A and draw a large arc.

  d Put the point of the compasses on the end of the line marked B and draw a large arc that crosses the other arc in two places.

  e Use a staight-edge to join the points where the two arcs cross with a straight line.

  f Check that your diagram looks similar to this:

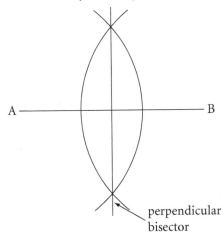

perpendicular
bisector

2 Follow these instructions to draw the midpoint of a line segment CD.

  a Draw a line segment 6 cm long. Label one end C and the other end D.
     Make sure you allow at least 10 cm of space above and below the line for drawing the arcs.

  b Open your compasses to a radius of 7 cm.

  c Put the point of the compasses on the end of the line marked C and draw a large arc.

  d Put the point of the compasses on the end of the line marked D and draw a large arc that crosses the other arc in two places.

  e Place your straight-edge along the line joining the points where the two arcs cross.

  f Mark a small dot where straight-edge crosses CD.

  g Check that your diagram looks similar to this:

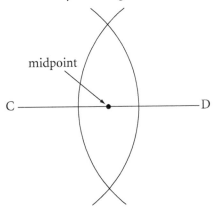

midpoint

  h Check this is the midpoint by using a ruler to measure the distance from C to the midpoint and D to the midpoint. They should both be 3 cm long.

3 This is part of Jake's homework.

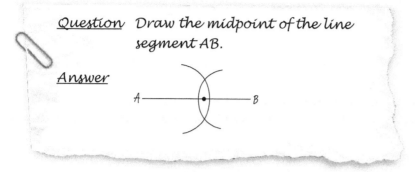

Question Draw the midpoint of the line segment AB.

Answer

He has used compasses and a ruler, but he has made a mistake.
  a What do you think he has done wrong?
  b Explain how you think he made this mistake.

4 a Using a ruler and protractor, draw a rectangle with a base of 10 cm and height of 6 cm.

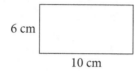

6 cm

10 cm

  b Using compasses and a straight-edge, draw on your diagram the midpoints of all four sides.
  c Join your midpoints, in order, with straight lines.
  d Using compasses and a straight edge, draw on your diagram the midpoints of all four of these new sides.
  e Join these new midpoints, in order, with straight lines.
  f What do you notice about this new shape?

◆ Exercise 12.3 Drawing an angle bisector

1 Follow these instructions to draw the angle bisector of angle ABC.
  a Draw a line 7 cm long and label it AB.
  Use a protractor to measure an angle of 60° from B.
  Draw another line 7 cm long to complete the angle.
  Label the end of the line C.
  Your diagram should look like this:

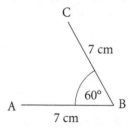

C

7 cm

60°

A

B

7 cm

  b Open your compasses to a radius of about 4 cm.
  c Put the compass point on the angle at B and draw an arc that crosses AB and BC.
  d Put the compass point on the point where the arc crosses AB and draw an arc in the middle of the angle. Do the same from the point where the arc crosses BC.

e Join point B to the point where the two arcs cross, in the middle of the angle.
Use a straight-edge to draw a straight line.
Your diagram should look like this:

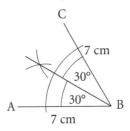

f Use a protractor to check that the angle bisector is accurate by measuring the two smaller angles.
They should both be 30°.

2 a Draw an angle ABC. It can be any size between 20° and 90°, except 60°.
Make sure the arms of the angle (AB and BC) are between about 5 cm and 8 cm long.
   b Using only compasses and a straight-edge, draw the angle bisector of angle ABC.
   c Use a protractor to check that your angle bisector has cut your angle exactly in half.

3 a Draw an angle DEF. It can be any size between 100° and 170°.
Make sure the arms of the angle (DE and EF) are between about 5 cm and 8 cm long.
   b Using only compasses and a straight-edge, draw the angle bisector of angle DEF.
   c Use a protractor to check that your angle bisector has cut your angle exactly in half.

4 The diagram shows a landing sector for the javelin-throwing event on an athletics field.
The javelin must land anywhere between the arms of landing area, shaded in light grey.
The angle between the arms of the landing area is 29°.
Andreas is practising throwing the javelin.
He wants to count how often the shot lands in each of the two halves of the landing area.

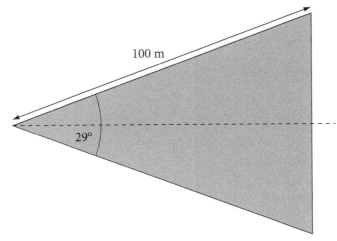

a Make an accurate scale drawing of the landing sector for the javelin.
b Draw on your diagram the angle bisector, shown by the dotted line.
Use only compasses and a straight-edge.
c Use a protractor to check that you have drawn the angle bisector accurately.

◆ Exercise 12.4 Constructing triangles

1 Make an accurate copy of each of these triangles.

a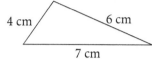

b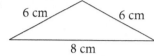

c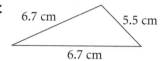

2 Make an accurate copy of each of these triangles.

a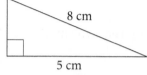

b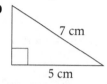

c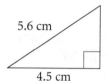

3 Use only compasses and a ruler for this question.
Set your compasses to a radius of 6.5 cm. Draw a circle with a
diameter of 13 cm.
Draw a diameter of the circle. This is a line across the circle passing
through its centre. Label this line segment AB.

a Make an accurate copy of triangle ABC in the top part of the circle.
Use the diameter AB as the base.

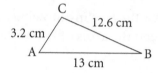

b Now make an accurate copy of triangle ABD in the bottom part of the circle.
Again, use the line segment AB as the base.

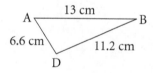

c What do you notice about both of your triangles?
Use a protractor to help you decide.

4 a Use the same method as in question **3** to make an
accurate copy of this diagram.

b What do you notice about both of your triangles?
Use a protractor to check.

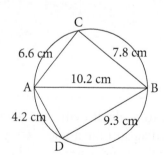

13 Graphs

1 a Copy and complete this table of values for $y = x - 4$.

x	−2	−1	0	1	2	3	4	5
y	−6							1

  b Draw a pair of axes. Use values of x from −2 to 5 and values of y from −6 to 3.

  c Draw a graph of $y = x - 4$.

2 a Copy and complete this table of values for $y = 2x + 3$.

x	−3	−2	−1	0	1	2	3	4
y	−3							11

  b Draw a pair of axes. Use values of x from −3 to 4 and values of y from −3 to 11.

  c Draw a graph of $y = 2x + 3$.

3 a Copy and complete this table of values for $y = 5 - x$.

x	−2	−1	0	1	2	3	4	5	6
y	7			4					−1

  b Draw a pair of axes. Use values of x from −2 to 6 and values of y from −1 to 7.

  c Draw a graph of $y = 5 - x$.

4 a Copy and complete this table of values for $y = 3x - 1$.

x	−3	−2	−1	0	1	2	3
y	−10			−1			

  b Draw a pair of axes. Use values of x from −3 to 3.

  c Draw a graph of $y = 3x - 1$.

5 a Copy and complete this table of values for $y = -0.5x$.

x	−4	−3	−2	−1	0	1	2	3	4
y	2							−1.5	

  b Draw a graph of $y = -0.5x$.

6 a Copy and complete this table of values for $y = -x - 1$.

x	−4	−3	−2	−1	0	1	2	3	4
y	3			0		−2		−4	

  b Draw a graph of $y = -x - 1$.

7 a Draw up a table of values of $y = 3x$. Use values of x between -3 and 3.
b Use the table of values to draw a graph of $y = 3x$.

8 a Draw up a table of values of $y = 1.5x + 1$. Use values of x between -4 and 4.
b Use the table of values to draw a graph of $y = 1.5x + 1$.

Exercise 13.2 Equations of the form $y = mx + c$

1 a Copy and complete this table of values for $y = 20x$.

x	−4	−3	−2	−1	0	1	2	3	4
y	−80					20			

b Copy the pair of axes.
c Draw a graph of $y = 20x$.

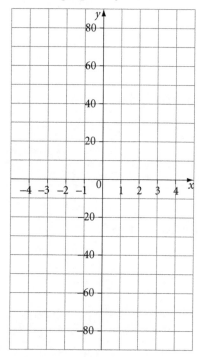

2 a Copy and complete this table of values for $y = 4x + 8$.

x	−4	−3	−2	−1	0	1	2	3	4
y	−8				8				24

b Copy the axes below.
c Use the table to draw a graph of $y = 4x + 8$.

3 a Copy and complete this table.

x	−4	−3	−2	−1	0	1	2	3	4
$2x + 3$	−5				3				11
$2x − 2$	−10				−2				6

b Draw a pair of axes with values of x from −4 to 4 and values of y from −10 to 11.
c On the axes draw the line $y = 2x + 3$.
d On the same axes draw the line $y = 2x − 2$.
e $(30, a)$ is on the line $y = 2x + 3$ and $(30, b)$ is on the line $y = 2x − 2$.
   Find the values of a and b.

4 a Copy and complete this table of values for $y = −0.1x$.

x	−40	−30	−20	−10	0	10	20	30	40
y	4								

b Use the table to draw a graph of $y = −0.1x$.
c The point $(36, c)$ is on the line. Find the value of c.
d The point $(−125, d)$ is on the line. Find the value of d.

5 a Copy and complete this table of values for $y = 8x − 16$.

x	−4	−3	−2	−1	0	1	2	3	4
y	−48				−16				16

b Use the table to draw a graph of $y = 8x − 16$.

◆ Exercise 13.3 The midpoint of a line segment

1 A is the point $(−4, 0)$, B is the point $(8, 0)$ and C is the point $(0, −6)$.
Find the coordinates of the midpoint of:
   a AB   **b** BC   **c** CA.

2 Find the midpoint of the line segment joining:
   a $(4, 2)$ and $(10, 12)$ **b** $(5, −3)$ and $(−3, −7)$ **c** $(−6, 8)$ and $(8, −6)$.

3 ABCD is a rectangle.

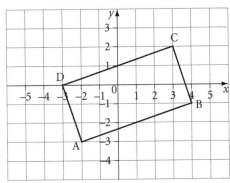

   a Find the midpoint of the line segment AC.
   b Show that the midpoint of the line segment BD is the same as the midpoint of the line segment AC.

4 A triangle has vertices at P(15, 25), Q(10, −15) and R(−20, −10).
Find the midpoint of each side of the triangle.

5 **a** Find the coordinates of the midpoint of AC.

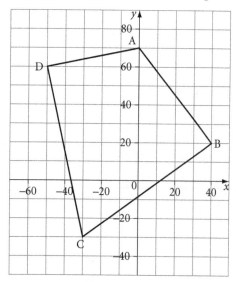

b Find the coordinates of the midpoint of BD.

6 A is the point (2.4, 6.2), B is the point (3.6, 2.4) and C is the point (−3.8, −1.4). Find:
a the midpoint of AB   **b** the midpoint of AC.

7 ABCD is a square. The coordinates of A are (−2, −6). The coordinates of C are (−3, −1).
Where is the centre of the square?

8 P is the point (0, 9) and the midpoint of PQ is (5, 7).
Find the coordinates of Q.

9 A is the point (16, 0) and B is the point (0, 8).
C is the midpoint of AB. D is the midpoint of BC. E is the midpoint of CD.
Find the coordinates of E.

◆ Exercise 13.4   Graphs in real-life contexts

1 The graph shows the speeds of a car and a van.

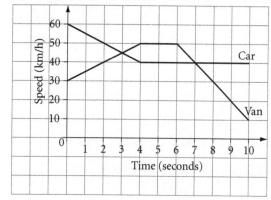

a What is the initial speed of the car?
b What is the highest speed of the van?
c For how long (in seconds) is the van travelling faster than the car?

2 The graph shows the journey of a car and a coach (bus) between Easton and Weston.

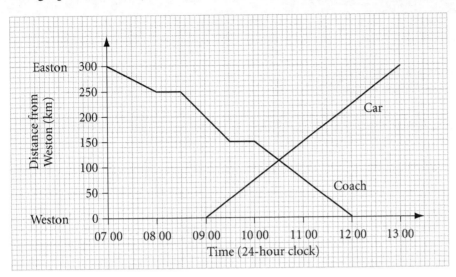

    a How many times does the coach stop on the journey?
    b How long does the car take to travel from Weston to Easton?
    c What time does the car pass the coach?
    d How far from Easton does this happen?

3 Asif is running to keep fit. He runs 6 km at a constant speed and takes 40 minutes.
    a Show Asif's run on a graph. Plot time on the horizontal axis and distance on the vertical axis.
Nawaz starts his run from the same point 10 minutes later and runs 6 km in 25 minutes along the same route.
    b Show Nawaz's run on the same graph.
    c How far did Nawaz run before he overtook Asif?

4 The speed of a car steadily decreases from 60 km/h to 30 km/h over 8 seconds.
    a Show this on a graph. Plot time on the horizontal axis and speed on the vertical axis.
A second car starts from rest and at the end of 8 seconds is travelling at 50 km/h.
    b Show the second car's speed on the same graph.
    c When are the two cars travelling at the same speed? What is that speed?

14 Ratio and proportion

◆ **Exercise 14.1   Simplifying ratios**

1   Simplify these ratios
   a 3:9   **b** 2:18   **c** 5:40   **d** 3:12   **e** 6:18
   f 7:21   **g** 10:2   **h** 27:3   **i** 30:3   **j** 16:4
   k 55:11   **l** 220:20   **m** 700:10   **n** 10:700   **o** 10:10

2   Simplify these ratios
   a 6:8   **b** 8:12   **c** 12:15   **d** 15:25   **e** 25:35
   f 35:56   **g** 32:24   **h** 27:24   **i** 36:24   **j** 40:24
   k 60:24   **l** 660:240   **m** 300:40   **n** 40:300   **o** 30:400

3   Simplify these ratios.
   a 2:10:12   **b** 8:12:16   **c** 8:4:10
   d 25:30:10   **e** 32:8:64   **f** 36:9:15

4   Simplify these ratios.
   a 250 m:1 km   **b** 2 m:15 cm   **c** $1.26:60 cents
   d 2.4 kg:600 g   **e** 1 minute:42 seconds   **f** 1.75 t:500 kg

5   Simplify these ratios.
   a 400 m:0.8 km:60 m   **b** 4 l:2200 ml:0.8 l   **c** $\frac{1}{2}$ hour:1 minute:20 seconds

   d 45 cents:$0.15:$2   **e** 6 m:0.09 km:300 cm   **f** 48 cm:88 mm:0.4 m

6   Simplify these ratios.
   a 0.4:2   **b** 2.5:5   **c** 0.8:3.2
   d 0.5:2.5   **e** 3.6:1.8   **f** 2.1:1.5
   g 2.5:6   **h** 2.1:1.4   **i** 0.05:0.3:1

> Remember to multiply by 10 or 100 first, to get rid of the decimal fractions.

7   Oditi and Dakarai are baking a huge cake.
   They mix 450 g of butter with 550 g of sugar and 1.1 kg of flour.

> The ratio of butter to sugar to flour is 4:5:11.

> The ratio of butter to sugar to flour is 45:55:11.

   Is either of them correct? Explain your answer.

8 Abbie is trying to find the quickest way to drive to her new job.
She tries three different routes and writes down how long each one takes.

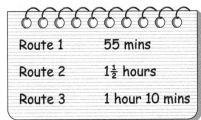

Route 1	55 mins
Route 2	1½ hours
Route 3	1 hour 10 mins

   a Abbie thinks that the ratio of her times for routes 1, 2 and 3 is 5:6:7. Without doing any
      calculations, explain how you know that Abbie is wrong.

   b Abbie's mum uses this method to work out the ratio of Abbie's times.

> *Route 1 : Route 2 : Route 3*
> *55 mins : 1 hour 10 mins : 1½ hours*
>   *0.55 : 1.1 : 1.5*
> *Multiply by 100:   55 : 11 : 15*
> *Divide by 5:   11 : 2 : 3*

      Explain the mistakes that Abbie's mum has made.

   c Work out the correct ratio of Abbie's times.

◆ Exercise 14.2   Sharing in a ratio

1 Share these amounts among Xavier, Razi and Shen in the given ratios.
   a $90 in the ratio 1:3:5   **b** $240 in the ratio 3:4:5
   c $1000 in the ratio 3:5:2   **d** $350 in the ratio 5:2:7

2 Greg, Harry and Ian share their electricity bill in the ratio 2:4:5.
   How much does each of them pay when their electricity bill is:
   a $110   **b** $165   **c** $352?

3 A city-wide gardening club is made up of men, women and children in the ratio 5:4:11.
   Altogether there are 2240 members of the gardening club.
   a How many members of the gardening club are:
      i men   **ii** women   **iii** children?
   b How many more men than women are there in the gardening club?
   c How many more children than men are there in the gardening club?

4 A box of chocolates contains milk, white and dark chocolates
   in the ratio 5:1:2.
   The box contains 56 chocolates altogether.
   a How many chocolates in the box are:
      i milk   **ii** white   **iii** dark?
   14 of the chocolates have been eaten.
   There are now 42 chocolates left in the box.
   b The ratio of the number of milk, white and dark
      chocolates in the box is changed to 4:1:2.
      How many chocolates in this box are:
      i milk   **ii** dark?

> Remember that there are
> not 56 chocolates in the
> box now, there are 42.

5 Alton, Dianne, Fredda and Nia run their own business.
They share the money they earn from a project in the ratio of the number of hours
they worked on the project.
This is the time-sheet for one of their projects.

> *Project earnings: $750*
> *Time spent working on project:*
> *Alton   5 hours   Dianne   12 hours*
> *Fredda   4 hours   Nia   9 hours*

How much does each of them earn from this project?

6 Four children inherit a painting.
They decide to sell it and share the money in the ratio of their ages.
The children are 6, 8, 11 and 13 years old.
The painting sells for $4750.

How much does each of them receive?

7 Greg, Nigel and Mike buy a boat.
The information shows how much each of them paid towards the boat.

> <u>*5th August 2012*</u>
> *Greg paid:*   *$1400*
> *Nigel paid:*   *$1050*
> *Mike paid:*   <u>*$1750*</u>
> *Total cost of boat:*   *$4200*

Five years later they sell the boat for $3300.
They share the money from the sale of the boat in the same ratio as they paid for the boat.
a How much does each of them receive from the sale of the boat?
b How much more money did Mike lose from the sale of the boat than Greg?
c Who made the smallest loss from the sale of the boat? How much did he lose?

8 At the start of every year Patrick shares 280 sweets between his children in the ratio of their ages.
This year the children are aged 3, 7 and 10.
How many <u>fewer</u> sweets will the oldest child receive in five years' time, than she received this year?

9 Toni, Lucca and Giovanni buy a house for $120 000.
Toni pays $10 000, Lucca pays $70 000 and Giovanni pays the rest.
Five years later they sell the house for $210 000.
They share the money in the same ratio that they paid for the house.
How much profit does Giovanni make on the sale of the house?

◆ Exercise 14.3   Solving problems

1   Four cups cost $8. Work out mentally the cost of:
    a one cup   **b** five cups   **c** eight cups.

2   The cost of two cakes is $5. Work out the cost of:
    a one cake   **b** three cakes   **c** nine cakes.

3   A gardener is paid $54 for six hours' work.
    Work out mentally how much the gardener is paid for four hours' work.

4   Here are the ingredients for a Swiss roll cake.

Swiss roll cake (serves 6)

72 g plain flour   6 ml baking powder

72 g castor sugar   3 eggs

Work out mentally how much of each ingredient is needed to make a Swiss roll
cake that serves:
    a 24   **b** 9   **c** 15.

5   Ahmad and Alicia share some sweets in the ratio 2:3.
    Ahmad gets 14 sweets.
    a How many sweets does Alicia get?
    b How many sweets do they share?

6   A meat pie contains chicken and turkey in the ratio 4:1.
    The pie contains 300 g of chicken.
    a How much turkey is in the pie?
    b How much meat is there altogether in the pie?

7   Three children share some sweets in the ratio of their ages.
    The children are four, seven and nine years old.
    The oldest child gets 54 sweets.
    a How many sweets do the other children get?
    b How many sweets do they share?

 8   Mia makes a cold drink she calls iced punch. She uses vanilla ice cream, grape juice and ginger
    ale in the ratio 1:4:5.
    Mia has plenty of vanilla ice cream, but only 2250 ml of grape juice and 2750 ml of ginger ale.
    She makes as much iced punch as she can with these ingredients.
    How much of each ingredient does she use?

 9   Bikka makes some brown paint.
    He mixes blue, yellow and red paint in the ratio 2:5:6.
    He uses 250 ml of yellow paint.
    How much brown paint does he make?

Blue paint   Yellow paint   Red paint   Brown paint

15 Probability

◆ **Exercise 15.1   The probability that an outcome does not happen**

1 These are the probabilities for some severe weather in the next month.

Event	Hurricane	Earthquake	Flooding	High temperatures
Probability	0.2	0.05	0.1	0.7

Find the probability that there will not be:
a a hurricane   **b** high temperatures   **c** flooding   **d** an earthquake.

2 The probability that Hassan will not be late for school tomorrow is 95%.
What is the probability he <u>will</u> be late for school tomorrow?

3 Seb estimates these probabilities for his total time running in a marathon.

Time	Under 3 hours	3 to $3\frac{1}{4}$ hours	$3\frac{1}{4}$ to $3\frac{1}{2}$ hours
Probability	0.1	0.6	0.25

Find the probability that Seb will take:
a 3 hours or more   **b** more than $3\frac{1}{2}$ hours

4 The probability that a team will reach the semi-finals in a competition is 0.6.
The probability that the team will reach the final is 0.3.
The probability the team will win the final is 0.2.
Find the probability that the team will:
a not reach the semi-finals   **b** not reach the final   **c** not win the final.

5 If you throw two dice, the probability that the numbers are the same is $\frac{1}{6}$. The probability
of getting two sixes is $\frac{1}{36}$. Find the probability of:

a the two numbers being different   **b** not getting two sixes.

6 A spinner has ten sectors in different colours. The sectors are different sizes. Here are the
probabilities of scoring three of the ten colours:

Colour	Red	Blue	Yellow
Probability	0.1	0.2	0.05

The spinner is spun. Find the probability that the colour is:
a not red   **b** not red or blue   **c** not red or blue or yellow.

7 Athletic and United are playing a game of football. The probability that Athletic will win is 0.1. The probability that United will win is 0.6. Find the probability that:

a Athletic will not win   **b** United will not win   **c** the game will be a draw.

8 The table shows the possible delay in a flight taking off from an airport.

Flight departure	On time	Up to 30 minutes late	30 minutes to one hour late
Probability	60%	25%	10%

Find the probability that the departure is:

a late   **b** more than 30 minutes late   **c** more than one hour late.

◆ Exercise 15.2   Equally likely outcomes

1 Mia writes the numbers from 1 to 20 on separate cards. She chooses a card at random. What is the probability that the card is:

a 13   **b** not 13   **c** a number less than 13   **d** a factor of 20   **e** a prime number?

2 Six cards show a square, a rectangle, an isosceles triangle, an equilateral triangle, a rhombus and a parallelogram. One card is chosen at random. Find the probability that it shows a shape with:

a four sides   **b** four equal sides   **c** straight sides   **d** all the angles equal.

3 This is a calendar for August one year.

Monday	Tuesday	Wednesday	Thursday	Friday	Saturday	Sunday
				1	2	3
4	5	6	7	8	9	10
11	12	13	14	15	16	17
18	19	20	21	22	23	24
25	26	27	28	29	30	31

a Tanesha chooses one day at random. Find the probability that she chooses:

i a Sunday   **ii** a Monday   **iii** a Thursday or Friday   **iv** not a Tuesday.

b She chooses a Friday in August at random. Find the probability that it is:

i the 8th   **ii** not the 15th   **iii** before the 20th.

4 These are the prime numbers less than 50.

a Alicia writes the numbers from 1 to 50 on separate cards. She chooses one card at random. Find the probability that it is:

2 3 5 7 11 13 17 19 23 29 31 37 41 43 47

i a prime number   **ii** a prime number less than 20   **iii** an even prime number.

b If the number is a prime, what is the probability that it is:

i less than 25   **ii** more than 30   **iii** an even number?

5 A random number generator generates a whole number in the range 1 to 100.
   a What is the probability it is 40 or more?

   b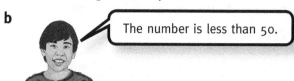

   The number is less than 50.

   Now what is the probability it is 40 or more?

   c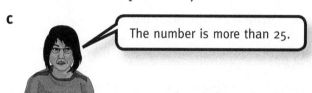

   The number is more than 25.

   Now what is the probability it is 40 or more?

6 There are five girls and three boys in a group. The teacher chooses one person at random.
   a How could the teacher make a random choice?
   b What is the probability that the choice is: **i** a girl   **ii** a boy?
   The teacher chooses a boy. The teacher then chooses a second person at random.
   c What is the probability that the second person is: **i** a girl   **ii** a boy?

7 Anders flips two coins. Explain why the probability of two heads is $\frac{1}{4}$.

8 A teacher wants to choose a student at random. The teacher decides to choose the first person
   to walk through the classroom door at the start of the lesson.
   a Explain why this is not a good method.
   b Suggest a better method.

◆ Exercise 15.3   Listing all possible outcomes

1 Carlos has four notes in his wallet: $5, $10, $20 and $50. He takes out two notes at random.
   a There are six possible pairs of notes. List them.
   b Find the probability that:
      i one of the notes is $5   **ii** the total value of the notes is more than $50.

2 Two three-sided spinners each have the numbers 1, 2 and 3 on them.
   a Draw a table to show the different possible totals when the spinners are spun together.
   b Find the probability that the total is:
      i 3   **ii** 4   **iii** an even number   **iv** 9.
   c Draw a table to show the different possible products of the
   two numbers.

   > Remember that the product is the result of multiplying two numbers.

   d Find the probability that the product is:
      i 3   **ii** 4   **iii** an even number   **iv** 9.

3 Sasha throws two normal six-sided dice and finds the difference between the two numbers scored.
   a Draw a table to show the possible differences between the two numbers.
   b Find the probability that the difference is:
      i 0   **ii** 1   **iii** 2   **iv** 5.

4 Alicia, Maha and Zalika are girls. Xavier and Razi are boys. They enter a competition. A girl came first and a boy came second.
   a List all the possible pairs for first and second.
   b Find the probability that:
     i Alicia was first and Razi was second   **ii** Maha was first   **iii** Xavier was second.

5 Shen and Tanesha each choose a number.

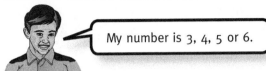
My number is 3, 4, 5 or 6.

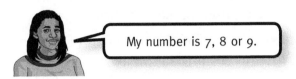
My number is 7, 8 or 9.

   a Copy and complete this table to show the possible totals of the two numbers.

+	3	4	5	6
7				
8		12		
9			14	

   b Find the probability that the total is:
     i 12   **ii** 13 or more   **iii** 10   **iv** less than 10.
   c Draw a similar table to show the difference between the two numbers.
   d Find the probability that the difference is:
     i 1 or 2   **ii** 3 or 4   **iii** 6
   e Find the probability that the product of the two numbers is more than 30.

6 One fair spinner has three equal sections coloured red, yellow and green.
Another fair spinner has three equal sections coloured red, green and black.
Xavier spins both spinners.
   a Show all the possible outcomes in a table.
   b Find the probability that:
     i both spinners show red   **ii** just one spinner shows red
     iii the spinners show different colours.

◆ Exercise 15.4   Experimental and theoretical probabilities

1 Dakarai has made a spinner with four sections coloured green, blue, red and yellow. He wants to test whether it is fair.
He spins it 20 times and gets these results.

Colour	Green	Blue	Red	Yellow
Frequency	3	8	5	4

   a Find the experimental probability for each colour after 20 throws.
   b Do you think the spinner is biased? Give a reason for your answer.

Dakarai spins the spinner another 80 times. Here are the results of all 100 spins.

Colour	Green	Blue	Red	Yellow
Frequency	24	35	17	24

   c Find the experimental probability for each number after 100 throws.
   d Do you think the spinner is biased? Give a reason for your answer.

2 Oditi wants to see if she can flip a coin fairly.
She flips a coin 200 times and records the number of heads after every 50 throws.

Spins	50	100	150	200
Frequency of heads	29	54	79	107

   a Find the experimental probability for heads after 50, 100, 150 and 200 throws.
   b Is Oditi throwing the coin fairly? Give a reason for your answer.

3 Anders wants to find the probability of scoring a total of at least 20 when he throws six dice.
   a What are the smallest and largest possible totals when six dice are thrown?
   Anders runs a computer simulation and gets these results.

Number of throws of 6 dice	50	100	200	300	400	500
Frequency of 20 or more	26	57	119	186	245	311

   b Work out the experimental probability of scoring a total of at least 20 after 50, 100, 200, 300, 400 and 500 throws.
   c Use your values to estimate the theoretical probability of scoring a total of at least 20.

4 'If you drop a piece of buttered bread it is more likely to land buttered side down.'
Hassan does an experiment to test this statement. He wants to estimate the probability that the bread will land buttered side down. Five people each drop a piece of bread 20 times.

Person dropping bread 20 times	A	B	C	D	E
Number of times buttered side down	16	18	14	15	12

   a Explain why dropping the bread 20 times is not enough to give a reliable estimate.
   b Combine all the results to get an experimental probability based on dropping the bread 100 times.

The five people repeat the experiment to get these results.

Person dropping bread 20 times	A	B	C	D	E
Number of times buttered side down	15	14	10	12	19

   c Find an estimate based on all the results so far.
   d Why is the answer to part **c** the most reliable estimate?

16 Position and movement

◆ Exercise 16.1 Transforming shapes

1 Copy each diagram. On your copy, reflect the shape in the mirror line with the given equation.

> When you copy a diagram to transform a shape, be sure to leave enough space to complete the transformation.

a

mirror line $y = 4$

b

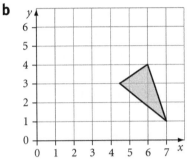

mirror line $x = 4$

c

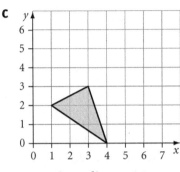

mirror line $y = 3.5$

2 Copy each diagram. On your copy, draw the image of the object using the translation given.

a

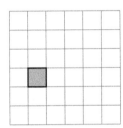

3 squares right
2 squares up

b

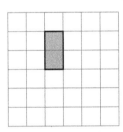

2 squares left
3 squares down

c

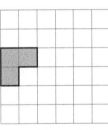

4 squares right
1 square down

d

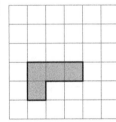

1 square left
3 squares up

3 Copy each diagram. On your copy, use the information you are given to rotate the shape.

a

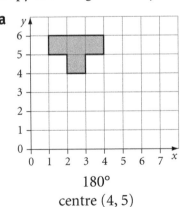

180°
centre (4, 5)

b

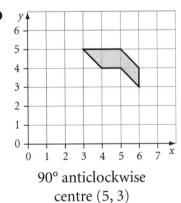

90° anticlockwise
centre (5, 3)

c

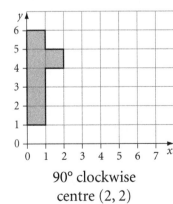

90° clockwise
centre (2, 2)

4 Copy the diagram.

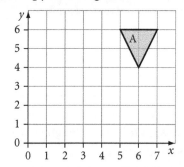

Draw the image of A after each combination of transformations.

a A translation 4 squares left and 1 square up followed by a reflection in the line $y = 4$. Label this image B.

b A rotation of 90° anticlockwise, centre (5, 4) followed by a translation 3 squares down. Label this image C.

c A reflection in the line $x = 5$ followed by a rotation of 180°, centre (5, 3). Label this image D.

 5 Zalika and Ahmad are discussing this diagram.
It shows two shapes, A and B.

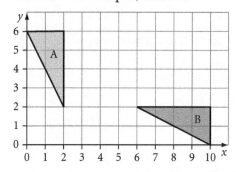

I can transform shape A to shape B by reflecting it in the line $x = 3$ and then rotating it 90° clockwise, centre (4, 2).

I can transform shape A to shape B by rotating it 90° anticlockwise, centre (4, 4) and then reflecting it in the line $x = 6$.

Is either of them correct?
Draw diagrams to explain how you worked out your answer.

6 The diagram shows five triangles, A, B, C, D and E.

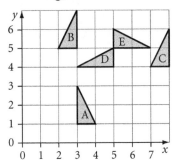

Look at each of the four transformations described below.
Name the object triangle and the image triangle for each transformation.
   a A reflection in the line $x = 4$, followed by a translation 3 right and 3 up.
   b A rotation 180°, centre (3, 3) followed by a reflection in the line $y = 5$.
   c A translation 2 left and 1 down, followed by a rotation 90° anticlockwise, centre (2, 3).
   d A rotation 90° clockwise, centre (3, 5), followed by a translation 2 right.

◆ Exercise 16.2   Enlarging shapes

1 Copy each of these shapes onto squared paper.
   Enlarge each one using the given scale factors.
   The centres of enlargement are marked
   with dots.

> In this exercise, when you copy a shape onto squared
> paper, leave plenty of space all around it. Otherwise,
> you may not have enough room to enlarge it.

   a scale factor 2   **b** scale factor 3   **c** scale factor 4

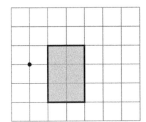   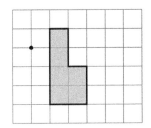   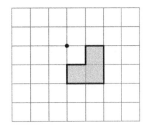

   d scale factor 2   **e** scale factor 3   **f** scale factor 2

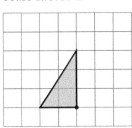   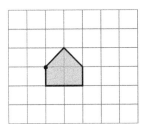   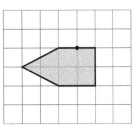

   g scale factor 2   **h** scale factor 3   **i** scale factor 2

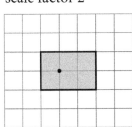   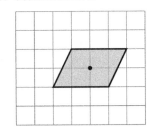   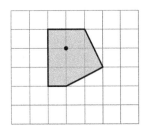

2 The vertices of this triangle are at $(2, 1)$, $(2, 4)$ and $(4, 2)$.

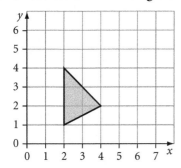

a Copy the diagram onto squared paper.
Mark with a dot the centre of enlargement at $(1, 2)$.
Enlarge the triangle with scale factor 2 from the centre of enlargement.

b Write down the coordinates of the vertices of the image.

3 The vertices of this parallelogram are at $(1, 5)$, $(3, 3)$, $(5, 3)$ and $(3, 5)$.

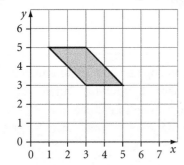

a Copy the diagram onto squared paper.
Mark with a dot the centre of enlargement at $(2, 5)$.
Enlarge the parallelogram with scale factor 2 from the centre of enlargement.

b Write down the coordinates of the vertices of the image.

4 The vertices of this trapezium are at $(2, 2)$, $(3, 2)$, $(5, 4)$ and $(2, 4)$.

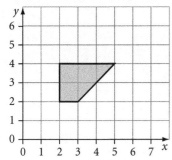

a Copy the diagram onto squared paper.
Mark with a dot the centre of enlargement at $(3, 3)$.
Enlarge the trapezium with scale factor 2 from the centre of enlargement.

b Write down the coordinates of the vertices of the image.

5 The diagram shows four objects, A, B, C and D and their images after enlargement.
For each object, write down the coordinates of the centre of enlargement, and the scale factor.

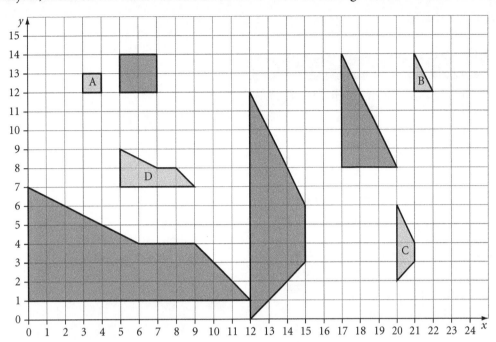

17 Area, perimeter and volume

◆ Exercise 17.1   The area of a triangle

1 Work out the area of this right-angled triangle.

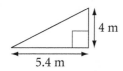

2 Work out the area of each of these triangles.

a 7 m, 12.8 m

b 95 cm, 200 cm

3 A triangle has a base length of 15.4 cm.
   The area of the triangle is 65.45 cm².

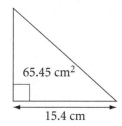

Dakarai works out that the perpendicular height of the triangle is 4.25 cm.
   a Without using a calculator, explain how you can tell that Dakarai is wrong.
   b Work out the perpendicular height of the triangle.
   c What mistake do you think Dakarai made?

◆ Exercise 17.2   The areas of a parallelogram and trapezium

1 Work out the area of each of these parallelograms.

a 8 mm, 20 mm

b 8.4 cm, 3.4 cm

2 Work out the area of each of these trapeziums.

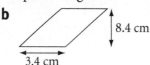

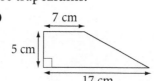

a 4.8 m, 2.6 m, 3.4 m

b 7 cm, 5 cm, 17 cm

3 Here are four shapes A, B, C and D.

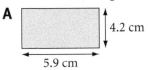

A 4.2 cm
5.9 cm

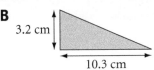

B 3.2 cm
10.3 cm

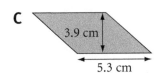

C 3.9 cm
5.3 cm

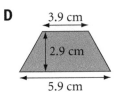

D 3.9 cm
2.9 cm
5.9 cm

Here are five area cards.

i 14.21 cm²   **ii** 16.48 cm²   **iii** 18.41 cm²

iv 20.67 cm²   **v** 24.78 cm²

  a Using only estimation, match each shape to its area card. Show your working.
  b Use a calculator to check that you have matched the shapes and the area cards correctly.
  c Which area card did you not use?

4 A parallelogram has an area of 43.4 cm².
It has a perpendicular height of 28 mm.

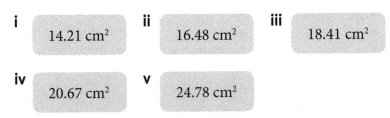

Area = 43.4 cm²   28 mm
? mm

What is the length of the base of the parallelogram?

5 The diagram shows a trapezium with an area of 7182 mm².

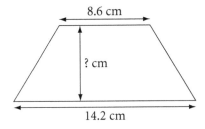

8.6 cm
? cm
14.2 cm

What is the perpendicular height of the trapezium?

◆ Exercise 17.3   The area and circumference of a circle

Use π = 3.14 for all questions in this exercise.

1 Work out the circumference of each circle.
Round your answers correct to 1 decimal place.
a radius = 10 cm   **b** diameter = 10 m   **c** diameter = 5 cm

2 Work out the area of each circle.
Round your answers correct to 1 decimal place.
a radius = 5 cm   **b** diameter = 5 m   **c** diameter = 1 cm

3 Work out the area of each semicircle.
Write down all of the digits on your calculator display.
a radius = 6 cm   **b** diameter = 6 m   **c** diameter = 3 cm

4 Work out the perimeter of each semicircle.
Write down all of the digits on your calculator display.
a radius = 6 cm   **b** diameter = 6 m   **c** diameter = 3 cm

5 Work out the perimeter of each quadrant.
Round your answers correct to 1 decimal place.
a radius = 5 m   **b** diameter = 6 cm   **c** diameter = 7 mm

> A quadrant is a quarter of a circle.

6 The diagram shows a semicircle and a quadrant.

 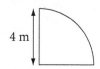

> I think the area of the semicircle is less than the area of the quadrant.

Is Maha correct? Show working to support your answer.

7 The diagram shows a semicircle and three-quarters of a circle.

> I think the perimeter of the semicircle is less than the perimeter of the three-quarter circle shape.

Is Jake correct? Show working to support your answer.

1 Copy and complete the working to calculate the area of each compound shape.

a

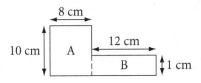

Area A = $l \times w$ = 8 × ☐ = ☐
Area B = $l \times w$ = 12 × ☐ = ☐
Total area = ☐ + ☐ = ☐ cm²

b

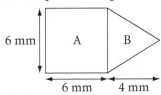

Area A = $l \times w$ = ☐ × ☐ = ☐
Area B = $\frac{1}{2} \times b \times h = \frac{1}{2}$ × 6 × ☐ = ☐
Total area = ☐ + ☐ = ☐ mm²

2 On each of these compound shapes, work out:
  i the missing lengths   **ii** the area of the shape.

a

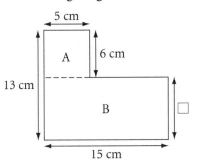

b

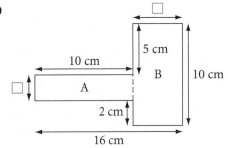

3 Work out the area of each compound shape.

a

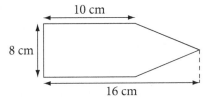

b

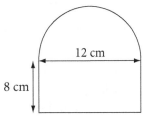

4 Xavier drew these three shapes.

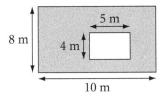

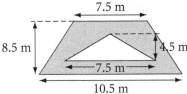

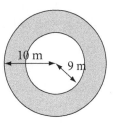

The shaded areas in these three shapes
work out to be the same size!

Is Xavier correct?
Show clearly how you worked out your answer.

1 Work out the volume of each cuboid.

a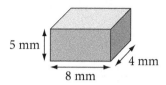

5 mm
4 mm
8 mm

b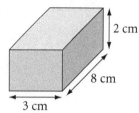

2 cm
8 cm
3 cm

c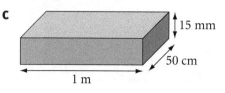

15 mm
50 cm
1 m

2 Work out the surface areas of each cuboid.

a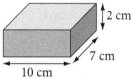

2 cm
7 cm
10 cm

b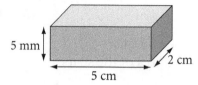

5 mm
2 cm
5 cm

c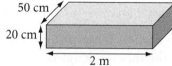

50 cm
20 cm
2 m

3 The table shows the volume and dimensions of some cuboids.

	Length	Width	Height	Volume
a	5 cm	6 cm	2 cm	
b	20 mm	10 mm		1200 mm³
c		3 m	6 m	72 m³
d	8 cm		8 cm	256 cm³
e	5.2 m	7.3 m		379.6 m³
f		12 mm	8 cm	288 mm³

Copy the table and fill in the missing values.

 4 The diagram shows a cuboid.
The length of the cuboid is 22 mm.
The width of the cuboid is 8 mm.
The volume of the cuboid is 880 mm³.
  a Work out the surface area of the cuboid.
  b Use estimation to check your calculations to part **a**.

8 mm
22 mm

 5 The diagram shows a cuboid.
The width of the cuboid is 25 cm.
The end face of the cuboid is a square.
The volume of the cuboid is 1.25 m³.
  a Work out the length of the cuboid.
  b Work out the surface area of the cuboid.

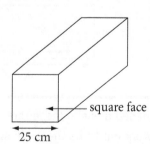

square face
25 cm

1 For each solid:
  i sketch a net of the solid   **ii** work out the surface area of the solid.
  a triangular prism (right-angled triangle)   **b** triangular-based pyramid (all triangles equal in size)

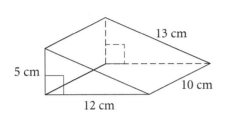

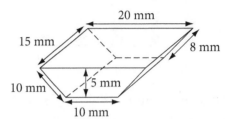

  c square-based pyramid (all triangles equal in size)   **d** trapezoidal prism

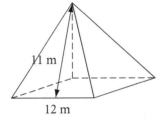

> 'Trapezoidal' means that
> the end is a trapezium.

 2 Razi thinks that the triangular prism has a smaller surface area than the cube.
Use estimation to decide whether Razi is correct.

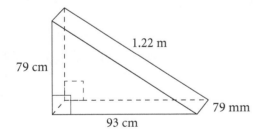

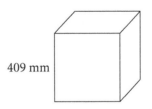

 3 Mia draws a cube of side length 35 mm.
She also draws an isosceles triangular prism with the dimensions shown.

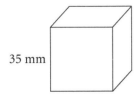

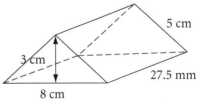

Mia thinks that the cube and the triangular prism have the same surface area.
Is Mia correct? Show clearly how your worked out your answer.

18 Interpreting and discussing results

◆ **Exercise 18.1 Interpreting and drawing frequency diagrams**

1   The frequency diagram shows the number of homeworks given to students from class 8B in one week.

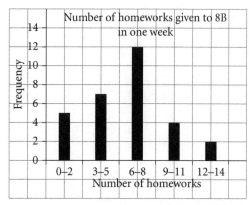

   a How many students were given 6–8 homeworks?
   b How many more students were given 0–2 homeworks than were given 12–14 homeworks?
   c How many students are there in class 8B?

2   The frequency diagram shows the heights, in centimetres, of some plants.
   a How many plants were between 20 and 30 cm tall?
   b What was the tallest possible plant shown?
   c Fewer plants were between 0 and 10 cm tall than were between 10 and 20 cm tall. How many fewer?
   d How many plants were grown altogether?

3   The frequency table shows the number of breakfasts sold each day in a café during one month.

Number of breakfasts sold	Frequency
0–9	1
10–19	3
20–29	7
30–39	11
40–49	5

   a Draw a frequency diagram to show the data.
   b How can you tell that the person that made the frequency table has made a mistake? Explain your answer.

c The manager of the café says: 'The frequency diagram shows that the greatest number of breakfasts sold was 49.'
Is the manager correct? Explain your answer.

d On how many days were at least 20 breakfasts sold? Explain how you worked out your answer.

4 The frequency table shows the heights of sunflowers grown in class 8V's biology lessons.

Height of sunflowers, h (m)	Frequency
$1.0 < h \le 1.2$	2
$1.2 < h \le 1.4$	3
$1.4 < h \le 1.6$	6
$1.6 < h \le 1.8$	12
$1.8 < h \le 2.0$	5

a Draw a frequency diagram to show the data.

b The tallest student in class 8V is 1.6 m. How many sunflowers are taller than the tallest student?

c Hassan says: 'The frequency diagram shows that the shortest sunflower was only 1 m high.'
Is Hassan correct? Explain your answer.

d Tanesha says: 'The frequency diagram shows that the tallest sunflower was exactly 2 m high.'
Is Tanesha correct? Explain your answer.

e How many sunflowers were grown in class 8V's biology lessons?

◆ Exercise 18.2 Interpreting and drawing pie charts

1 The table shows the desserts chosen by the 40 customers in a restaurant one evening.

Dessert chosen	Ice cream	Cheese cake	Pavlova	Fruit salad	None
Number of customers	9	12	5	8	6

a Draw a pie chart to represent the data.

b What percentage of the customers did not have a dessert?

2 The table shows the results of a survey about students' favourite weekdays.

Favourite weekday	Monday	Tuesday	Wednesday	Thursday	Friday
Number of students	5	8	14	6	27

a How many students participated in the survey?

b Draw a pie chart to represent the data.

c What fraction of the students most liked Mondays?

3 Greg owns a bicycle shop. The pie chart shows Greg's sales of four different BMX bike models in October.

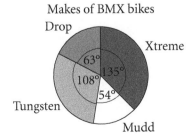

Makes of BMX bikes

Altogether Greg sold 200 BMX bikes in October.

a Which model of BMX bike was the most popular?

b What fraction of the bikes sold were Mudds?

c What percentage of the bikes sold were Tungstens?

d How many of the bikes were Xtremes?

4 Tom carried out a survey to find some students' favourite types of holiday.
He recorded the results in a pie chart, like this.

Students' favourite type of holiday

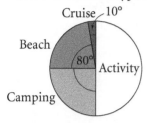

a What fraction of the students preferred activity holidays?

b 20 students preferred cruise holidays.

   i How many students preferred activity holidays?

   ii How many students preferred beach holidays?

   iii How many students took part in the survey?

5 A group of men and women took part in a survey about favourite types of holiday.
The pie charts show the results.
The group was made up of 180 men and 240 women.

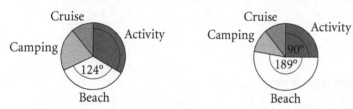

Mens' favourite types of holiday   Womens' favourite types of holiday

a How many women preferred activity holidays?

b How many men preferred activity holidays?

c How many more women than men said they preferred beach holidays?
Show how you worked out your answer.

d The 'Cruise' sector for men and women is the same size in both pie charts.
Without doing any calculations, explain how you know that more women than men preferred
cruise holidays.

◆ **Exercise 18.3   Interpreting and drawing line graphs**

1 The line graph shows how many drawing pins a company produced over a six-year period.

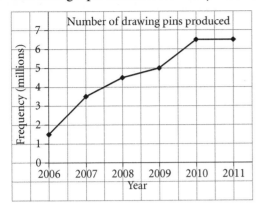

   a How many drawing pins were made in:
     i 2009   **ii** 2010?
   b In which year did the company make 3 500 000 drawing pins?
   c Between which two years was the greatest increase in production?
   d Between which two years was there no increase in production?
   e Between which two years was the smallest increase in production?
   f Describe the trend in the company's production over the six-year period.

2 Kelly records the rentals of skis at her shop each month for one year.
The data is shown in the line graph.

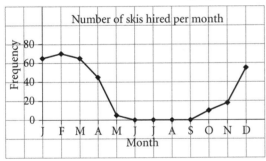

   a Approximately how many skis did Kelly rent in:
     i March   **ii** July?
   b In which month did she rent the most skis?
   c Between which two months did her rentals triple?
   d Describe the trend in ski rentals over the year.

3 The table shows the average price of books sold from 'Brendan's Books' over a 20-year period.

Year	1990	1994	1998	2002	2006	2010
Average price of book ($)	11.10	10.80	8.20	7.00	7.30	12.50

   a Draw a line graph to show the data.
   b Describe the trend in the data.
   c In which four-year period did the price of books change the most?
   d Use your graph to estimate the average price of books sold from 'Brendan's Books' in 1996.

Exercise 18.4 Interpreting and drawing stem-and-leaf diagrams

1 The stem-and-leaf diagram shows how long, to the nearest minute, it took students from class 8U to complete their homework.

Key: 2 | 3 means 23 minutes

```
2 | 3   5   7   9
3 | 0   2   5   5   5   7   8   9   9
4 | 1   2   4   6   7   9
```

a How many students timed their homework?
b What was the shortest time taken to complete the homework?
c How many of the students took longer than 30 minutes?
d Work out:
    i the mode   **ii** the median   **iii** the range of the data.

2 The stem-and-leaf diagram shows the playing times, to the nearest minute, of some films.

Key: 10 | 2 means 102 minutes

```
10 | 5   7   8
11 | 3   3   3   5   7   8   9
12 | 0   2   4   5   6   7   8   8
13 | 3   5   7   7
```

a How many films were timed?
b How long was the shortest film, in minutes?
c How many of the films lasted less than 2 hours?
d How many of the films lasted more than 2 hours?
e Why is your total for parts **c** and **d** together not the same as your answer for part **a**?
f Work out:
    i the mode   **ii** the median   **iii** the range of the data.

3 These are the masses, in grams, of 25 newborn mice.

6.4 7.3 6.4 8.9 6.9 7.8 6.0 6.2 8.5 7.1 5.9 7.2 8.0

9.5 8.2 5.9 7.5 6.4 7.3 8.6 5.8 9.2 6.9 6.1 9.0

a Draw an ordered stem-and-leaf diagram to show this data.
b How many of the mice weighed less than 8 g?
c What fraction of the mice weighed more than 9 g?
d What percentage of the mice weighed between 6.3 and 7.9 g?
e Use your stem-and-leaf diagram to work out:
    i the mode   **ii** the median   **iii** the range of the data.

4 These are the masses, in kilograms, of the motorbikes on sale in a showroom.

| 162 | 180 | 175 | 172 | 198 | 165 | 175 | 208 | 188 | 176 | 166 | 200 |
| 179 | 208 | 194 | 170 | 180 | 189 | 190 | 173 | 207 | 199 | 209 | 175 |

  a Draw an ordered stem-and-leaf diagram to show this data.
  b How many motorbikes are there in the showroom?
  c How many of the motorbikes are heavier than 200 kg?
  d What fraction of the motorbikes are lighter than 180 kg?
  e What percentage of the motorbikes are 190 kg or heavier?
  f Use the stem-and-leaf diagram to work out:
    i the mode   **ii** the median   **iii** the range of the data.
  g What is the mean mass of the motorbikes on sale in the showroom?

◆ Exercise 18.5   Drawing conclusions

1 Dion makes wooden animals. He sells them on the internet.
The stem-and-leaf diagram shows the prices of the wooden animals he sells in one week.

Key: 28 | 50 means $28.50
```
28 | 50  50  50  75  75  99
29 | 00  00  50  50  99  99  99
30 | 00  25  50  50  50  50
31 | 50  75  75  90  90  99
```

Dion is happy with his profit if the mean price is greater than $30.00.
Is Dion happy with his profit this week?
Show your working.

2 Alyson and Haito both play basketball.
They each take five shots at the basket for practice and count how many times they score.
They do this 20 times each.
The bar graphs show the number of times they score out of their five shots.

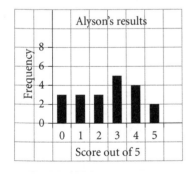 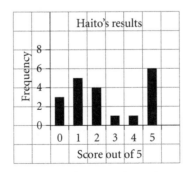

Alyson thinks that she scored more times out of her five shots, on average, than Haito.
  a Explain how Alyson can be right.
  b Explain how Alyson can be wrong.

3 In their PE lesson, the students in class 8P did two gym obstacle courses.
The frequency diagrams show the times taken by the students to complete the two courses.

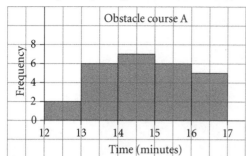
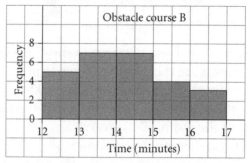

a How many students did the two gym obstacle courses in their PE lesson?

b Which course seems the easier to complete? Explain your answer.

Mr Pym, the PE teacher, says: 'If 60% of you finish the course in less than 15 minutes, you can all go early for lunch.'

c Does the class go early for lunch if Mr Pym uses the times from gym obstacle course A? Show your working.

d Does the class go early for lunch if Mr Pym uses the times from gym obstacle course B? Show your working.

e Do class 8P go early for lunch if the PE teacher uses all 52 times from gym obstacle courses A and B? Show your working.

4 A jewellery shop keeps a record of the number of silver and gold necklaces they sell each week.
The line graph shows the number of necklaces they sold during a ten-week period.

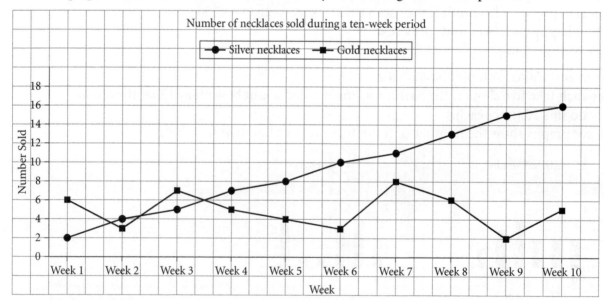

a Describe the trend in the sales of
   i silver necklaces.
   ii gold necklaces.

b How many silver necklaces do you think the shop will sell in week 11? Explain your answer.

c How many gold necklaces do you think the shop will sell in week 11? Explain your answer.